SuperQuickLessons

5 *Proven Skills of*
BUSINESS
SUCCESS

"...take a 'big bite' out of this book!"

Harvey Mackay

author of the #1 New York Times bestseller
Swim with the Sharks Without Being Eaten Alive

Randy Clay's SuperQuickLessons™ 5 Proven Skills of BUSINESS SUCCESS

ISBN #0-9725246-2-2
Copyright © 2006 Randall A. Clay
PCI Press
P.O. Box 361
Sand Springs, OK 74063

Randy Clay's SuperQuickLessons,
SuperQuickReminders,
SuperQuickRecommendations,
SuperQuickEndorsements are registered trademarks of PCFI, Inc.

Library of Congress Cataloging-in-Publishing Data

Clay, Randall 1961

      Randy Clay's SuperQuickLessons^{TM} *5 Proven Skills of* BUSINESS SUCCESS
      Randy Clay
      International Standard Book Number 0-9725246-2-2
      1. Success in Business 2. Sales & Marketing
       3. Management & Leadership I. Title

Printed in the United States of America

10 9 8 7 6 5 4 3 2 1

Randy's
SuperQuickEndorsements ™

"Randy Clay has gone from a 'one-man show' to successful business owner for one simple reason - he had the sense to look for sound business advice and then follow it. If you are running a business take a big bite out of this book!"

Harvey B. Mackay

author of five New York Times bestsellers including
Swim with the Sharks Without Being Eaten Alive
www.mackay.com

*"Loved the book!
An easy read with practical advice.
Every lesson proves that Randy's ideas
really work!"*

Patricia Fripp, CSP, CPAE

Award Winning Speaker - Executive Speech Coach - Author
www.fripp.com

"Randy truly knows that the ability to sell is the #1 skill in both business and life; therefore, the lessons in his book are important to learn so you can profit and build successful teams."

Blair Singer

Rich Dad's Advisor and Author of New York Times bestsellers,
Sales Dogs & The ABC's of Building a Business Team that Wins
www.salesdogs.com & www.sp-ww.com

*"Randy is as good a student as he is a teacher.
After reading this book I can't wait to see what
SuperQuickLessons he's got coming next!"*

Tom Antion

Nationally Acclaimed Speaker & Author of the bestseller
The Ultimate Guide to Electronic Marketing for Small Business
www.antion.com

Randy's SuperQuickEndorsements ™

"The advice in Randy's book, SuperQuickLessons
5 Proven Skills of Business Success, is simple, easy to understand,
practical, and it WORKS. Don't miss out -- you must get
your hands on this gem of a book, SuperQuick!"

Alexandria K. Brown

The "E-zine Queen", Internet Entrepreneur and Marketing Coach
www.ezinequeen.com

"I've been promoting and marketing best-selling authors,
Fortune 500 CEOs, and celebrities for 16 years,
but I learned some new strategies from
Randy Clay that should double my success!"

Brian Feinblum

Chief Marketing Officer
Planned Television Arts in New York
www.plannedtvarts.com

"This is simply a smashing book, chock-full of practical,
easy to implement strategies that will boost your career
and grow your bottom line."

Myra Golden

President and Senior Trainer
Myra Golden Seminars
www.myragolden.com

"Would you like to get right to the heart of
building a successful business ?
Read Randy's book and buy a copy for everyone on your team,
and just hope that your competition doesn't read it first!"

Frank F. Lunn

President of the Kahuna Business Group
& Author of the bestseller *Carpe Aqualis!- Seize the Wave*
www.kahunaworld.com

Contents

"Believe It or Not, The Next Level Of Your Success Is Hidden In Somebody's Book!"

It was a Sunday morning in the spring of 1990. Personally, I thought it was going to be just another day that started by taking my young family to church. I remember that it had been a difficult week at my screen printing business. In the hall outside the church auditorium, I was visiting with a fellow entrepreneur about some of the management challenges I was having with one of my employees. Really, and to be honest I wasn't just visiting with my friend, I was whining.

I found myself not having any answers on how to handle a disgruntled employee and how to keep his dissatisfaction from spreading to the others on my very small team. I was beginning to wonder if not going to college was one of my biggest problems and if so, was I destined for failure?

When I finished describing my situation, he looked at me and told me about a chapter in a book that he had just finished titled, *"It Isn't the People You Fire Who Make Your Life Miserable, It's the People You Don't."* He continued to tell me that the name of the book was, *Swim with the Sharks Without Being Eaten Alive*, written by a man named, Harvey Mackay.

Even though my face said thanks for the recommendation, my mind put the thought of reading a boring business book way back on the shelf of my mind.

On the way out, as was my habit, I stopped by my pastor's office to say the usual, "great service," but this particular day he hadn't yet made it to his office. I noticed a book on his desk that wasn't a copy of the "good book" I had seen many times before. As I went over to get a closer look at the cover, you can only imagine my puzzled facial expression when I read, *Swim with the Sharks Without Being Eaten Alive*, complete with a picture of this Harvey Mackay guy.

You could call it an omen, a sign, or whatever you want, but my lightning-quick mind suggested that I read that book. After lunch, I went down to our local drug store and found a copy that looked just like the one I'd seen on the desk. I remember reading the first half that afternoon and finishing it later that evening. It's overall simplicity overwhelmed me, and it was the first business book that I had ever read that enabled me to apply its philosophies immediately.

The surprising thing, was the application of the principles that Harvey shared, actually produced results! I re-read that book so many times, that every sales negotiation or management situation that presented itself was handled with knowledge that I had embraced by learning the "Mackay Way." It revolutionized the way I thought about business and forever changed the way I conducted myself in the marketplace.

When I started my sign and decal company back in 1983, the only knowledge I had was the skill of how to produce a quality product. I had been married a little over a year and had just turned 22 years old. Most of my time was spent trying to convince potential clients that I could actually produce the signs or decals they were looking for. While most of my contemporaries were finishing up their degrees, I was enrolling in the School of Hard Knocks, and didn't even know it.

When I was working the "One-Man Show", things were great. I controlled everything, but as the business grew, I began to realize that I couldn't do this all by myself, and the need for different production equipment was going to be a necessity. I had no knowledge of finance, accounting, personnel management, hiring, sales, marketing, or any of the other requirements to build a long lasting business.

For the first 7 years, I felt as if I was drowning because of ignorance. I thought of going back to school, but by 1990 I had a toddler running around the house and a thrilled stay-at-home mom chasing him.

The biggest revelation I received after reading *Swim with the Sharks* was that even if I did go back to school, any knowledge I would acquire would come, in one form or another, from books. So, for the last fifteen years I have been a "continually educated student," using every form of business education material I could get my hands on.

A few years ago, I officially marked Harvey Mackay as my literary mentor. Since *Swim with the Sharks* came out in 1988, Harvey has written five other New York Times Bestsellers. I had the privilege to escort him for two days during his last book tour which I'll tell you about near the end of this book. During our time together, I heard him tell one of his young admirers at the book signing that if he read all his books he would have the equivalent of an MBA degree. I was glad to hear that because I've always thought about what it would be like to have an MBA degree and when I think of all that I've learned from his writings in conjunction with things I've experienced, I finally have the "degree". In fact I think I'll make myself a certificate and see if Harvey will sign it. Who knows?

Seriously, I hope this book will inspire you to realize that the knowledge you need to succeed is probably already recorded within the pages of someone else's experience.

My intent is to share how I applied the knowledge and the results I received.

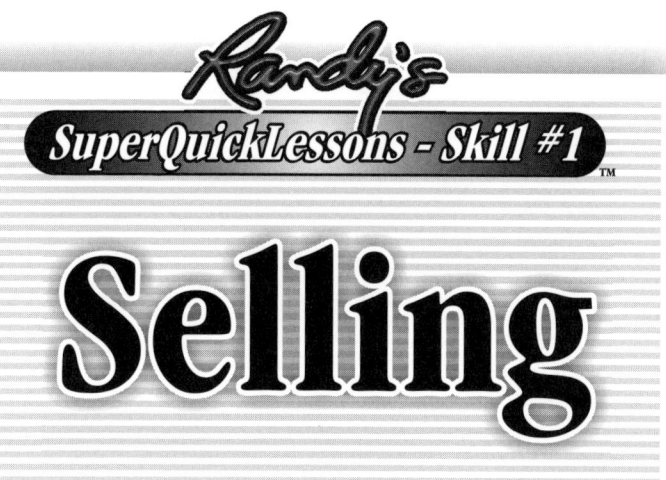

Randy's

SuperQuickLessons - Skill #1 ™

Selling

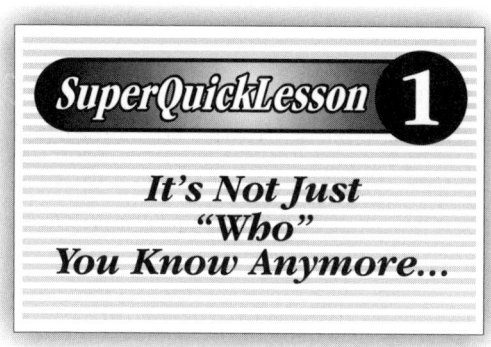

SuperQuickLesson 1

It's Not Just "Who" You Know Anymore...

The first thing I learned about selling from Harvey is that when it comes to buyers, they have been trained to keep the purse strings of the company well guarded, and some take on the task like a monster.

Cold call sales are the hardest in the world if you don't have the ability to respond correctly to rejection.

The thing that kept me going in the earlier years was that I refused to take rejection personally. I realized they weren't rejecting me, but the need for my product or service. How could they reject me, if they didn't know me?

Not long ago, I attended a half-day seminar with Patricia Fripp titled, *Getting, Keeping and Deserving Your Customers.* One of the clichés used in her seminar was, "It's not who you know, but who needs to know you!"

During one of the breaks, I visited with Patricia about what I had learned from Harvey to make a bigger impact in my sales career, by changing her cliché just a little. It goes like this: "It's not 'WHO' you know, but 'WHAT' you know, about who you know!"

As we continued to visit, I shared with her about my most important lesson on what is now called, "relationship selling." Before I could get the setting of the story out, she asked me to share my story with the group to help her make the point on how to deserve and keep a customer.

Back in the early '90s, there was an international drilling company I wanted for a client. I finally got the appointment to visit with the decision maker concerning the first product I wanted to sell. I offered to reproduce samples of their decals at no cost, in order to show an example of our quality and color matching ability.

The decision maker even sent me what I call the, "business love letter", stating their eagerness to visit again when I finished the samples.

At our next meeting, I'll never forget what was said. "Randy, your color matching and overall quality surpasses everything we've purchased in the past and even your pricing is below what we are currently paying, but we are going to stay with our current vendor."

I don't know about you, but if there was ever a time to take rejection personally, that would have been the time for me. Here I was, being led to believe that we were going to start dating, and I get dumped for an abuser.

It seemed like the only chance I had to get in the door and eventually sell them the safety signs they used on their fleet of oil drilling rigs.

I found myself rehearsing that meeting trying to figure out

what else I could have done to get that account.

One day, about two years later, I remembered a comment that was made in that rejection meeting.

Their company had safety representatives in different parts of the country and each one was responsible for purchasing signs for his or her own division of rigs. I made a phone call to the same buyer that shot down my first proposal, and asked a few simple questions:

Q. "Do your safety reps buy signs from catalogs?"

A. *"Yes, and they get catalogs from all over the country."*

Q. "Would it be possible to get their addresses to send them our sign information?"

A. *"Sure, what's your fax number?"*

Now, it's one thing to try and sell the tangible, face-to-face, but it's a totally different thing to sell the invisible over the phone. Just remember, it's more important to start a relationship than it is to close a sale. If you want to connect, you had better sharpen your conversational skills. Before I call a geographic area, I try to find out what's going on in the prospective buyer's world. I also look for any news that is related to their company. Get creative!

My first call was to Harrold in the Deep South. I introduced myself, letting him know who allowed me to call. I then took a few moments to visit about his career, how long he'd been with the company, and other things that would help me be sensitive to what his business and even personal needs were.

I told him thanks, and that I would send our sign

information right out.

Knowing that guys in the oil patch love hats, I also mentioned I would send him one of ours. At that time we had produced one of the most elaborate hats the oil industry had ever seen. Little did I know what chain of events that relatively inexpensive offer would start in the industry.

Harrold got all excited saying, he'd give the hat to his son, who had a collection of over five hundred hats. He had them cataloged and stored in special boxes. It became apparent I had just found a genuine oil patch hat collector. He listed a few hats his son had collected, and also mentioned a few he had been trying to find. There was one that he'd been looking for that caught my attention, it was Neal Adams Oil Well Firefighters in Houston.

When I hung up, I dialed the next number so fast I almost lost a fingernail. I was calling my good friend, Neal Adams. The next day, Neal's hats arrived and I stuck them underneath a couple of mine and off to Alabama they went.

Being that it only takes about two days to get a package to Alabama from Oklahoma, it shouldn't be hard to figure out what happened when that package reached his desk.

I love going to oil industry trade shows and seeing my buddy Harrold dragging another potential sign buyer to my booth. I never realized that those hats would create the best client/salesperson I've ever had.

SuperQuickReminders™

It's more important to build a relationship than it is to close a sale, on the first date!

Try to learn something from every rejection.

Listen for something that your client or prospect is excited about and make a note!

We all like buying from people we like. Become likeable!

SuperQuickRecommendations™

Swim with the Sharks
Without Being Eaten Alive
Short Course on Salesmanship Lessons 1-19
#1 Bestselling book by Harvey Mackay
Buy It...www.superquicklessons.com/harveyswim

Getting, Keeping, and Deserving Your Customers
Audio program by Patricia Fripp, CSP, CPAE
Buy It...www.superquicklessons.com/fripp

The One Minute Salesperson
book by Spencer M. Johnson, M.D. & Larry Wilson
Buy It...www.superquicklessons.com/spencersales

It's "All About Them"

The most common question I'm asked when visiting with a group of salespeople is, "How do you find information about a new or prospective client that you can use to make a long-lasting impression?"

Over the years, I've made it my No. 1 priority to learn as much as I can about the person I desire to do business with.

This philosophy comes from Harvey's Short Course on Salesmanship, Lesson No. 3. He says, *"Knowing something about your customer is just as important as knowing everything about your product."* I have found that one statement to be the most profitable one I've ever heard.

When it comes to actually finding out information, one of my favorite avenues is to first develop a relationship with the receptionist and/or the personal assistant to the person I'm wanting to reach.

You must realize that the receptionist is the guardian of the fort. He or she can make you or break you when it comes to making contact with the people you need to meet. I want to get to know the receptionist on a first name basis. I usually make small talk before asking to be put through to Mr./Ms. Prospect. I'll ask questions like, "How are things going with you today?" (A word of caution--you need to be prepared for anything, because the receptionist may let you know exactly how things are going.)

Once, after asking that question, my soon-to-be phone buddy let me know that her son was in an auto accident the night before, and even though he was going to be all right, her emotions were completely worn out. Naturally, I spent a few extra minutes encouraging her. Keep this in mind, people can tell if you really care about them, and really caring is the key to developing relationships.

If I get someone that I can tell has a fun personality, I'll say things like, "It's hotter than blazes out today. Do they have the air conditioner vent pointed in your direction? If not, connect me with maintenance and I'll get that taken care of for you." That one usually gets a laugh and an immediate connection to Mr./Ms. Prospect or at least their assistant.

Personally, I really enjoy working with executive assistants because they've been hired to get things done, and they've proven to me that they can.

Sooner or later, the building of these relationships will develop into a wealth of information that can help me WOW a prospect into a client.

Another favorite thing I do is what I call the, "It's All About Them" lunch. This is where I go to lunch and try not to mention anything about my products or services, instead I want the prospect to tell me about him or herself.

I usually start by asking something like, "Tell me, are you originally from (whatever city we are having lunch in)?" That is usually all it takes to get someone going.

One lunch I will always remember was with the safety director from a large company here in Tulsa. He told me he was from Kansas and was transferred when the company he was working for was purchased by one here in Oklahoma. He was really enjoying telling me about his high school football days and his favorite pro team. But the thing he was the most excited about was his ten year wedding anniversary the next week. He mentioned a great bed and breakfast he found just outside Oklahoma City, and that he and his wife were very excited to be able to get away for a few days. He told me that they were about to finish building their new house, and that his wife and children had been staying with her parents in another city. I could definitely understand his anticipation about their time together.

Surely, by now you can see an opportunity to make an impression and, believe me, I took it.

When I got back to the office I found the bed and breakfast on the Internet and gave it a call. I asked if there was someone locally that could make a fantastic gift basket for a couple celebrating an anniversary there next week. Of course, there was a company that could take care of me.

The week after the anniversary trip, I received the phone call. I loved the excitement in his voice as he told me that at first they thought this humongous basket of everything you could imagine was courtesy of the bed and breakfast--until his wife later read the card. They couldn't believe it!

Needless to say, I have sold tens of thousands of dollars worth of products to his company, and my initial investment was only a lunch and a $45 gift basket.

Another reason that I always emphasize the need to develop a relationship is because of what happened a few years after that first lunch.

One day I received a phone call letting me know that he had reached the top of the pay scale at his current company and was ready to look for another opportunity.

We started making phone calls to see who could get him the best opportunity first. I thought I had him an offer with one of my other clients but when we looked at the package he received from one of his phone calls, we decided he should go with his. In fact, the deal was so great, I was joking with him about quitting what I was doing and joining him. But there was only room for one.

With the sign ordering system we developed for him, I was pretty confident we could keep his former company's business. There is also nothing like having your client tell you that as soon as he's landed in his new office and assessed the situation he'll be calling to get a new program set up.

1st company he was with, $50,000+.

2nd company he went with, $100,000+?

One relationship,... priceless!

In reality, I ended up going with him after all.

SuperQuickReminders™

All receptionist's have the key to the front door!

Executive assistants are the GREATEST to work with. They get things done!

Use your memory only until you can find a pen!

If you truly focus on them, they'll find it hard to live without you!

SuperQuickRecommendations™

Swim with the Sharks Without Being Eaten Alive
Short Course on Salesmanship Lesson #4
The 66-Question Customer Profile
#1 Bestselling book by Harvey Mackay
Buy It...www.superquicklessons.com/harveyswim

Beware the Naked Man Who Offers You His Shirt
Short Course on Long-Term Sales Careers
Lessons 42-51
#1 Bestselling book by Harvey Mackay
Buy It...www.superquicklessons.com/harveyshirt

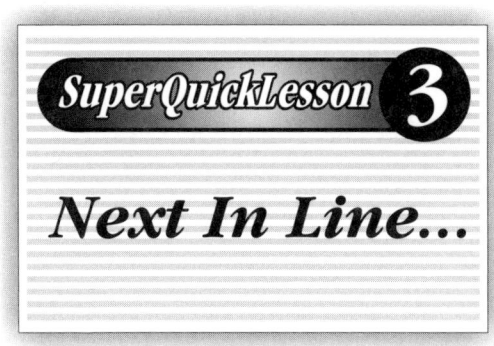

SuperQuickLesson **3**

Next In Line...

Another important thing I learned about being successful in sales, is that if you are not able to make a sale to a company you really want to do business with, the best place to find yourself, on their list of vendors, is No. 2.

Here's the truth: If you can get your name on enough lists in the No. 2 slot, sooner or later they will be calling. Now here's how I know this to be true...

Somewhere down the road, No. 1 is going to mess up, or your prospect will experience something that changes the way it does business. I can't number the times that I've had a call from someone saying something like: "Our senior buyer has just retired, and I'm kind of new in this position for buying safety signs. I've heard you have a better way of purchasing them than just digging through these catalogs all day." After I lock in the appointment and hang up the phone, the whole place can always hear me yell, "YAHOO!"

I found myself "next in line" with a company I had been wanting as a client, for over 8 years. (You read correctly, 8 loooooooooong years.)

One day out of the blue, they called saying that someone told them we could print, of all things, trash container decals, that remind people to keep their areas clean.

I had already done my homework about the company and knew enough about its production methods to have some suggestions ready that would help streamline the decal applications for its products. After waiting another year and staying in contact with the buyer, it finally happened.

In one of my, "just checking to see how you're doing", calls, I found out that the company was changing its logo and was sending the new decal project out for bid. I said that I would like to personally set up a time to visit about this new project. (When I hung up, again, my team heard another, "YAHOO!")

Knowing that it would be difficult to get the bid, because the previous vendor had been locked in for a zillion years, I had to come up with something that would put me on top.

There I sat with the materials manager, product manager, product engineer and a senior buyer. The meeting opened with the usual formal introductions and then we began discussing actual production of the new elaborate logo. I explained all the different ways we could do it. The thing I knew that would wake everyone up was when I said, "Would you like to see a production sample next week?" Before we wrapped up the meeting I began to ask some questions about how they applied the decals they needed for the daily quota of their products. I started out by asking, "Let me guess, do you have a wall in your plant that is covered with dozens of bins to hold each decal?"

Looking a little surprised by my question they answered, "yes". "And, does the person who applies the decals onto your equipment get a list of models that are to be shipped today?" Again, the answer was, "yes". "And, does that person go to those bins and hand count out each of the dozen decals that goes on each particular model?" Once again, "yes". (By this time they were looking at me like I was some kind of corporate spy.) My last question, "If we were able to furnish all your decals in a kit that would match a particular model number, would that help reduce overall production time?" Now for their first question. "You can do that?" My answer was, "absolutely"!

It was obvious however, that the engineer didn't seem very impressed or excited about being in the meeting in the first place, I knew I needed to make him an ally. He started mumbling that he wished someone would develop a small measuring unit that would be easier to affix to their products.

In addition to production samples of their new logo, you'll never believe what I took to that next meeting. In my hand was a prototype of that measuring device that he described the week before. His facial expression was priceless.

Just before it came time for the decision to award the contract, I asked if they had a trade show coming up. They answered, "Yes." I let them know that if they decided to award the contract to my company, I would be glad to mark their display units, new logo and all, absolutely **FREE**. Now, guess who got the contract?

SuperQuickReminders™

You never know what a friendly "How are ya?"
phone call will produce!

Do your homework,
they'll be impressed with what you know...
about them!

Always listen for the thing they would
least expect getting, and then get it!

It's amazing what the word FREE can do!

SuperQuickRecommendations™

Selling the Invisible
book by Harry Beckworth
Buy It...www.superquicklessons.com/harryselling

The Invisible Touch
book by Harry Beckworth
Buy It...www.superquicklessons.com/harrytouch

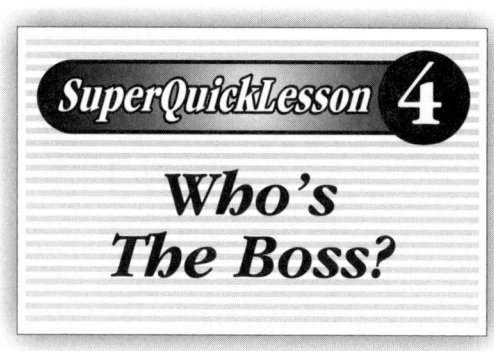

SuperQuickLesson 4

Who's The Boss?

Is it just me or has anybody else noticed that it seems like more people are giving a career in selling, a try? With all the layoffs that we've seen the last couple of years, I'm not surprised that people are stepping in to an arena that gives them a little more control of their destiny. Personally, I love seeing it!

A few years ago, I was attending a business building seminar in Dallas, Texas. One of the best speakers of the day was a sales expert named, Blair Singer. After his presentation, the group took a break. I went by his sales table just to observe the response of the crowd. At his book signing table was a small sign, maybe about 4 inches by 7 inches that I will never forget. The type read, "Those who can't sell, will always work for those who can." The second I read that simple statement, I said to myself, "ain't that the truth!"

Whether we realize it or not, the difference between the good life and a mediocre life, is your ability to sell. No matter what your occupation, marital status or parental status you are faced everyday with the need to sell.

I'm sure most everyone has had to sell the their ability to work, to a job interviewer. Remember how you had to sell your best characteristics to your spouse, back when you started dating? What a sales job that was! How about selling your kids the idea of a new vacation spot that doesn't sound so "GREAT" to them. You are selling all the time.

A few years ago, I developed a little program titled *10 Signs of a Super Salesperson*. One day, I was invited to a sales meeting for a national computer store, to do my presentation. My first question to a sales group is always, "Who's the Boss?" Almost every group will respond by pointing over to the sales manager or team leader.

I take them through a little exercise where we make a list after asking what qualities or characteristics that they like to see in the "Sales Boss". The list usually looks something like this.

Honesty (this is the #1 answer I get every time)
Someone that knows what they are talking about.
The ability to make quick decisions.
An encourager
A problem solver
Flexibility
Has integrity
Has negative emotions in control
Has a good sense of humor
Not a micro-manager
Not arrogant

After we finish writing them down, I will usually comment on how this list is very interesting because the qualities and characteristics mentioned are exactly the same ones that most consumers are looking for in a salesperson.

It's true! As a salesperson, the golden rule is #1. Treat others the way you want to be treated!

The next thing I share is that when you decide that you'd like to try a career in sales, you need to realize YOU are "THE BOSS"! In addition to all the qualities that most people list, that truly are vital to a successful sales career, you need to face the fact that you are the person in charge of whether you make it or not!

All the training in the world can't help a person that is not proactive in their desire to be a success.

Sales can be a tough career because of two simple reasons: No. 1. Some people are weak in people skills. If you don't care that much about meeting new people and striking up a simple conversation, you'll never make it.

No. 2. Some people can't separate the rejection of a product or service from themselves. They don't understand where self-esteem comes from.

If you can master these two reasons that most people fail in a sales career, the earning potential is as vast as the ocean.

And don't worry about those that are surfing the internet saying that we no longer need salespeople. There are plenty of consumers out there that still aren't comfortable on one of those electronic surf boards.

SuperQuickReminders ™

It's always been easier to sell the things people want, than to sell them the things they need, but sooner or later they are going to buy what they need!

Sales becomes enjoyable when YOU'RE convinced that you're selling the best product or service available.

Some salespeople are concerned that the internet will one day make them obsolete. If that does ever happen make sure you have a shop they can surf to.

SuperQuickRecommendations ™

10 Signs of a Super Salesperson (QuickRead E-Book)
by Randy Clay
Buy It...www.superquicklessons.com/supersales

SalesDogs
bestselling book by Blair Singer
Buy It...www.superquicklessons.com/salesdogs

SalesDogs Training School
Audio program by Blair Singer
Buy It...www.superquicklessons.com/dogtraining

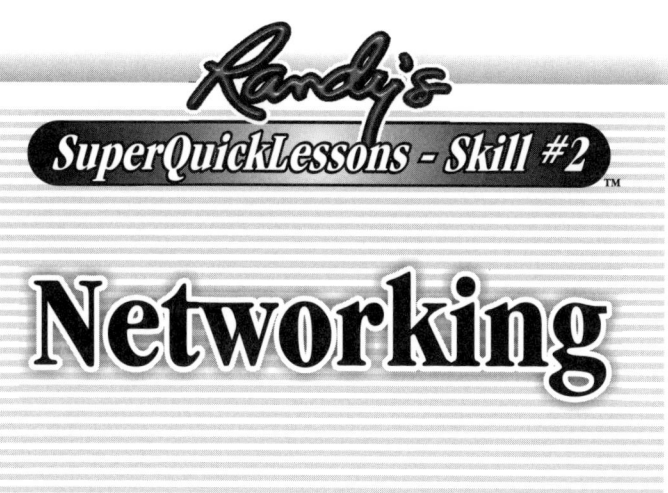

Randy's
SuperQuickLessons - Skill #2 ™

Networking

SuperQuickLesson 5

Networking Defined

I guess it's an addiction, every time I hear a business buzzword, I immediately wonder about it's origin.

Once, when I was in Plano, Texas displaying at an oil industry trade show, I overheard the salesman in the booth next to ours trying to give one of the conference attendees a lesson on networking. He was going on and on about developing relationships with people should have never been called networking, because networking is, "what you do with computers".

Even though I agree with the fact that the computer industry has chosen the word networking to describe a way that a series of computers could share information and communicate for the benefit of all who were connected together, I also realize that relationship networking or networking with people does the exact same thing.

Think about it for just a second. When people start networking together, they are really connecting up to share their information, resources and experiences.

Now, getting back to my curiosity of word origins, one day I started really thinking about the word, **Networking**. In the English language many of our words are compounded, which means, that we've combined the two words to better describe a picture we're trying to paint in the mind.

Look at the first word in the compound, "net". Realizing that a net has historically been a tool for gathering things, what kind of net quickly comes to mind when you hear or read the word "net"? (Hurry and get a type of net in your mind before reading on.)

When I share this word in my seminars, without fail the majority of the group says, "fish net". How about you? By chance, was that the type of net you thought of? It seems that, for some reason, the words, "fish" and "net", own a place in our minds that create a picture when we mention the word, "net".

Over the years, I have found that there is a comparison between net fishing and networking. Surprisingly there two simple things that you should know about net fishing that can make you a better networker.

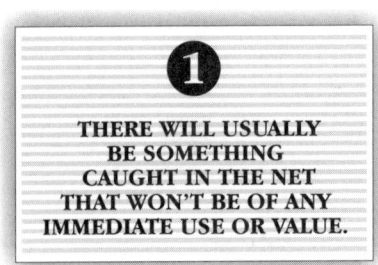

1

THERE WILL USUALLY BE SOMETHING CAUGHT IN THE NET THAT WON'T BE OF ANY IMMEDIATE USE OR VALUE.

I've found that no matter who I meet, whether it's one-on-one or at a social business function, every business card, brochure or introduction is important. When building a network of contacts you need to remember one extremely important thing. You are not building a network just for you. You are building it for everyone within your circle of influence.

Regardless as to whether or not the person or persons you have just met will be able to meet any immediate personal needs, you never have any idea of what that contact may offer in the future.

Here's a recent example to illustrate my point. Over the course of several months I kept running into a CPA at different chamber of commerce events in my city. The first time we met was at a meeting where I was asked to speak at our downtown library. After the meeting he introduced himself as a specialist in several areas pertaining to small business. Many of the areas he mentioned, I was very familiar with but I already had an accountant from way back. However, being that I practice what I preach, I put him in my network. About a year and a half later, I was in need of a little more tax advice than what I thought I was getting with my current accountant, and after seeing him at several other chamber events I finally stopped him one morning and asked him a few questions and believe it or not he gave me the answers I was looking for. He is the man that is going to take me and my companies to the next level.

My point is this, it makes no difference what you are thinking about the future relationship of the person you are currently meeting. Everyone is worthy to be added to your network in the beginning. Unlike commercial fishermen that have to throw back the ones they aren't fishing for, don't throw anybody out until you know for sure that they are not a good fit in your network.

The second thing you should know about net fishing is,

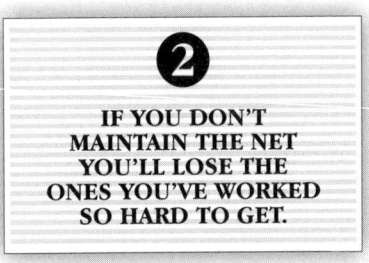

②

**IF YOU DON'T
MAINTAIN THE NET
YOU'LL LOSE THE
ONES YOU'VE WORKED
SO HARD TO GET.**

Another thing I've learned, is the importance of net maintenance. If you don't keep an eye on the net, holes can develop and result in losing a valuable catch.

Once you realize that your net is the most important tool for hanging on to your catch, you must also realize that you must make sure that your net is working to it's utmost potential.

In the next lesson, I share with you about the first net I used to make sure the "big ones" never got away. Regardless of which kind of net people think is the best, there is only one question that you need to answer...

IS YOUR "NET" WORKING?

SuperQuickLesson 6

My Personal
Wheel of Fortune

One of the oldest and simplest nets that have made millions of business people extremely successful, reminds me of a phrase connected with prime time television that has paralleled the subject of high finance. When a person has spoken these four simple words in this phase, followed by its corresponding action, one of three things will usually happen. They will stay where they are financially, increase financially, or lose everything that they have recently accumulated. The phrase is, "I think I'll spin." Untold millions of dollars have been won and lost by the action following this little phrase.

For decades, television viewers have shown their enthusiasm for America's number one prime time game show, Wheel of Fortune®.

Years ago, I found a wheel that is just as much fun and profitable as Pat and Vanna's, "Mega Spinner." Not only has it become a valuable part of my financial and social life, it has continued to grow every day for the last ten years. Believe it or not, I'm about to tell you about my Rolodex®.

One of the most valuable things I've been able to observe

and apply to my life, is learning how successful people are fanatics about meeting, staying in touch, and really developing human-to-human relationships. With all of the communication technology available today, I personally don't think anything can compare to the voice of someone you want to visit with.

Before the age of the electronic database, my Rolodex® would always be ready to make a difference in my day, and possibly in the day of someone I've taken an interest in. If I could only recall all the times I've been at my desk and said, "I think I'll spin," and without fail, I always find a few names in that fan of cards that I know could use a call from me. Whether it's a checkup on the latest family adventure, a quick reminder of who just turned a year older, or the traditional business call that turns into an actual addition to the monthly sales report, it's always a profitable visit. When calling a client, I never get tired of hearing him or her say, "I've been meaning to call you," or "Oh, my gosh! I was supposed to call you two weeks ago!"

When lecturing at universities about starting a Rolodex® file, I can almost hear the students saying, "come on Randy, step into the 21st century. A Rolodex® is a relic of history and the way of the future is the electronic database." Now, don't misunderstand, I'm as lap-topped and palm-piloted as the next guy, but the point I'm wanting to make is that it's not about the type of system you use, but how you take care of what the system represents.

In my Rolodex®, there are abundant opportunities to enhance my life in the area of financial and business wisdom.

It also contains a host of influences that promote a positive attitude about life in general. I get all of this with a simple spin and the realization that people are the only true fortune that I have.

I realize that a tremendous amount of today's commerce is done electronically by purchase orders, bank transfers, and now, online shopping. However, we need to always remember that behind every transaction, there is a "someone" that needs our product, service, or sometimes just an encouraging word.

The first article that I actually had published was a question and answer format. One of the questions asked, what was one thing I wish I had known when I started my company back in 1983. My answer was one that I learned from Harvey Mackay: "Most entrepreneurs need to realize the most important word in the English language for business people isn't even in the dictionary. It's spelled R-O-L-O-D-E-X.®"

SuperQuickReminders™

*A true Wheel of Fortune will never
have room for a space marked Bankrupt!*

*Fish just don't jump into the boat,
you've got to have something to
catch 'em with!*

*We've all heard about the one that got away.
If you're a <u>Pro</u> you'll find it doesn't happen...
very often!*

SuperQuickRecommendations™

Dig Your Well Before You're Thirsty
The <u>Only</u> Networking Book You'll Ever Need
#1 Bestselling book by Harvey Mackay
Buy It...www.superquicklessons.com/harveydig

**The Harvey Mackay
Rolodex® Network Builder**
by Harvey Mackay
Buy It...www.superquicklessons.com/harveyrolodex

SuperQuickLesson 7

Don't Wait For Them To Start The Conversation!

One of the greatest thrills I get is sharing with the beginner salesperson a few things that will put him or her ahead of the competition.

Several months ago, I had the opportunity to moderate a discussion at one of our Tulsa Chamber of Commerce Network Breakfasts.

I had submitted 3 questions that each table would discuss among themselves. The third question I came up with was based upon the need to help the freshman salesperson overcome the pull of the comfort zone. The question was, "How do you get from the comfort zone to the end zone?" With that question, I submitted a story about mastering the ability of talking to anybody at anytime.

Finishing a semi-weekly shopping tour through one of my favorite home improvement stores, I finally wound up at the checkout counter. In front of me was a man purchasing a bucket load of $50 gift cards. I couldn't help it. I tapped him on the shoulder and said, "Excuse me, but could you tell me what it would take to become one of your of your closest friends?"

When he looked at me, I was staring at the pile of cards on the counter. He busted up laughing and said that one of the guys at his office suggested these cards as a give-away for a golf tournament his company was hosting.

While we were waiting for his credit card company to be convinced that someone hadn't stolen his card for such a large purchase ($2500, if my memory serves me right), I caught a glimpse of a logo that was embroidered on his polo shirt. My lightening quick mental database recognized the logo as one of the companies we wanted to do business with. I quickly found out that he was the Senior Vice-President. What a coincidence!

After giving him my 60 second audiologo, we exchanged business cards. He told me to give him a call and he'd connect me with his purchasing manager. I'm still doing business with his company, and you should be convinced that if you've got something to sell, you need to get creative about how to start a conversation with the next person you meet.

There is never a day that goes by that I haven't tried to meet someone new, get to know something about that person and immediately add the name to my database.

One of my most memorable additions occurred during an afternoon of golf. My golf coach, Paul, and I had our tee time and were told we'd be paired up with another duo. Apparently the other two were running a little behind and just as I was about to attempt a swing, here they came.

After the introductions, I asked them to kindly look

the other way to hopefully keep myself from being totally embarrassed. They said, "Oh that's all right, we haven't played in months." I immediately thought, 'yeah right'-- it's probably because you're taking a break from the PGA tour.

In the usual, "what do you do" conversations, I learned that they were brothers and the owners of two very prominent restaurants in Tulsa.

Talk about two great guys--they spared no enthusiasm when I shot my first birdie ever. We were marching around the green giving high fives and the whole bit. What a day! The icing on the cake was when we exchanged business cards and a week later, I received a gift certificate to one of their restaurants.

The point of this little lesson is to remind you that everyone you meet is important and worth putting in your network. That same afternoon, I had my assistant enter them in my database. I called a few days later to thank him for the gift and told him to give me a call the next time they play.

Since that day on the course, one of the brothers has sponsored several of my networking seminars with lunch for the attendees. That golf day was truly a win/win.

Always remember, a contact file or database is profitless, unless it is used. I don't know about you, but maintaining my network is as important to me as my vehicle maintenance because I'm extremely dependent on both to get me somewhere in life.

Randy's SuperQuickReminders™

Whether you're a computer or a human, networking is the way to share all the good stuff you've got!

Nothing feels worse than needing a business card and discovering you left them at the office.

Striking up conversations is one skill you should never leave home without!

Randy's SuperQuickRecommendations™

How To Build A Network of Power Relationships
Audio Program by Harvey Mackay
Buy It...www.superquicklessons.com/harveyaudio

Cracking The Networking Code
*4 Steps to Priceless Business Relationships
book by Dean Lindsay*
Buy It...www.superquicklessons.com/netcode

SuperQuickLesson 8

Network Fitness Test

Back in the early '90s when I started my literary education with Harvey Mackay, the Rolodex® Corp. published a book titled, *The Harvey Mackay Rolodex® Network Builder.*

It was about 75 pages and the back dozen pages or so were preprinted Rolodex® cards that could be punched out and used to start a system similar to what Harvey described in his book.

The valuable tool I want to share was toward the end of the book and was a simple self-test that asked the question, How Good Are Your Network Building Skills?

If you're interested in starting a networking exercise program, grab a separate piece of paper, a pen or pencil and rate yourself on a scale of 1 to 5 on the following 12 questions. 1 being "not true" and 5 being "very true."

1. I have a large network of people I can call upon when I need helpful information or a resource. **1 2 3 4 5**

2. When I meet someone new, I record and file information about that person within 24 hours. **1 2 3 4 5**

3. I add somebody new to my database or contact file at least every week. **1 2 3 4 5**

4. I follow up with new contacts right away writing a note, making a phone call, or sending a clipping. **1 2 3 4 5**

5. I keep track of special things that matter to my contacts like their family, hobbies and achievements. **1 2 3 4 5**

6. I can easily find out when I was last in contact with someone. **1 2 3 4 5**

7. When mailing something out, a resume, sales letter, or a change of address, I always have correct name spellings, titles, addresses for everyone in my network. **1 2 3 4 5**

8. I know about and acknowledge special dates like birthdays, anniversaries and graduations. **1 2 3 4 5**

9. When I want to give a business gift, I can count on my database or contact file to provide me with an excellent idea of what a person might like. **1 2 3 4 5**

10. I make it easy for others to add me to their network by providing my business card, notifying them of address changes, and informing them about my career progress. **1 2 3 4 5**

11. When friends ask me for the name of a good resource, I have no trouble providing one. **1 2 3 4 5**

12. When the moment comes, I can really "wow" a customer, prospect or potential employer with special information or an idea that shows I care. **1 2 3 4 5**

Total the points above and score yourself:

0-24 You're in rough shape. It's time to make a change.

25-36 You're doing some things right. Now let's get to work.

37-44 You're off to a great start. Go-Go-Go!

45-55 You've got superstar potential. All you need is the polish.

56-60 You're already there. Keep up the great effort!

If you happen to see some weak areas and would like a few tips that will definitely enable you to "up your score", log-on to *www.superquicklessons.com/networkfit* to get a copy of my *QuickRead E-book* titled, *Networking Fitness Program.*

SuperQuickReminders™

*The first 3 habits of the test should be
as easy as making a decision to start
doing them.
(so go ahead and give yourself a 5 on each one)*

*Treat everyone you meet as though they
are valuable.
(Because they are!)*

SuperQuickRecommendations™

Network Fitness Program
(QuickRead E-Book)
by Randy Clay
Buy It...www.superquicklessons.com/networkfit

Masters of Networking
*book by Ivan R. Misner, Ph.D.
& Don Morgan M.A.*
Buy It...www.superquicklessons.com/mastersnet

Randy's

SuperQuickLessons - Skill #3 ™

Managing

Fixing The Boat While It's Still Afloat!

There is nothing quite like the feeling you get as you are sitting comfortably at your desk, when you notice a manager or employee standing in your doorway, white as a ghost and saying, "We have a little problem."

In the early years of my business career, my first thought after hearing those words was, "we" can't include "me", because I was just sitting here minding my own business.

But as the years pass, the realization becomes very clear, if you are at the helm of your ship, you'd better be ready when you get the report that someone just knocked a hole in the bottom of your boat. It shouldn't be too hard to figure out that if the boat you are responsible for is going down, you had better be proficient at taking quick and positive action, unless of course, you've somehow learned to walk on water.

I'll never forget one particular day, just like the one I've just described.

When I got the report of a problem, it was the only thing my production manager could get out of his mouth. It seemed like it took only an atomic second when my brain figured out what the only possible problem at the beginning of this major contract could be.

In less than 30 minutes the team had mistakenly produced more than 800 markings with a material cost of over $2000.

When my manager told me that the first person responsible was about to start crying, my thought was, "Tell him to hold up a minute and I'll be back there to join him." I was, however, surprised by such an emotional response, because in all the years I've operated this company I have never raised my voice, verbally abused or belittled an employee for a mistake they've made. I've also experienced that the majority of the time, my team members are usually harder on themselves than I would ever be.

I would like to submit the following tips for consideration the next time you have to correct a mistake with the goal of maintaining overall morale and productivity.

1. *Check your eyes for railroad ties!* When a team member makes a mistake it's usually because they overlooked something. Before you begin checking or trying to clear up their eyesight, make sure that you have a clear picture yourself and be absolutely sure that you personally didn't contribute to their inaccuracy. Things like incomplete information, ordering incorrect materials or supplies won't get you nominated for Manager of the Year.

2. *If you plan to use that pile of rocks on your desk, make sure your nameplate reads... "GOD"!* In ancient times stoning someone to death in public was the ultimate fix for mistakes.

Today, some managers get a high from throwing insults, hurling profanities and trying to belittle the mistake maker in front of their peers. Everyone of us has probably been in that situation and can still remember the embarrassment and humiliation that came with it. If you have to correct someone, do it privately and remember, team members will always produce better if they aren't concerned about dodging rocks.

3. *Know the difference between an Incident and a Problem.* This is an easy one. You'll find that an incident is usually something that has never happened this way before. Make sure everyone involved understands why it happened and always have a plan to keep it from possibly happening again. If you see an incident happen again and again, you now have a problem.

4. *Don't build memorials with the products of failure!* Going back to the day I started this lesson with, I knew that morale was the most valuable thing I couldn't afford to lose and stay on schedule. I wasn't able to re-cycle the material that was produced incorrectly. The material stood close to 3-feet high. I told my manager to remove the "monument" from the production area immediately. I didn't want any reminder staring the team in the face as they were trying to maintain productivity.

The best quote I've ever read on the importance of team morale sums it up for me: "It doesn't matter how many pails of milk you lose, as long as you don't lose the cow!"

SuperQuickReminders™

Your team is the mirror of your management style!

When you lose your emotional control, you are in danger of losing overall productivity. Both are difficult to get back!

Most people don't like to be constantly reminded of their mistakes, and they don't particularly care for the person reminding them either.

SuperQuickRecommendations™

The One Minute Manager
#1 Bestselling book by
Ken Blanchard, Ph.D. & Spencer Jonson, M.D.
Buy It...www.superquicklessons.com/oneminute

The Power Of Ethical Management
Bestselling book by
Ken Blanchard & Norman Vincent Peale.
Buy It...www.superquicklessons.com/ethical

SuperQuickLesson 10

The First Thing
You Should Know
About People

To be a good manager, the first thing you should know is, *"Most People Love to be **Recognized**."*

The reason that I put the word, "most", is because there are some people that don't really care one way or the other if they get any attention or not, but as a whole, most people do like a little recognition when it's due.

The reason I know this to be true is because you can see it on their faces. I've always equated a smile with being pleased.

There are times when I'm conducting a seminar or at a speaking engagement, and I see someone that may be of some notoriety or importance to me personally, I always make sure that I introduce them to the group.

If we think hard enough, all of us should be able to remember a time when we've received a little recognition and it brought a sense of importance. On the other hand, there have been times when you didn't get any recognition for something you accomplished and you can still remember the negative feeling it brought.

One Saturday, I was in a restaurant in a small city south of Tulsa with my brother. As we went up to the counter to pay, the woman taking our money asked,

"Aren't you Randy Clay?"

"It's me", I answered.

"I heard you speak at a chamber of commerce luncheon last year and really enjoyed your presentation," she said. "I also bought your book and wanted you to know that I really, really enjoyed it."

"Thank you very much and I really, really, appreciate you taking a moment to let me know," I replied. We spent a few minutes talking about the restaurant and how long she's been there and a few other things that I later recorded in her new database entry.

My brother mentioned that it was, "pretty cool" that she remembered me and had obviously read my book. I have to be honest that her comments really helped my ego. I really enjoy hearing that I've made a contribution and somebody's better for it. Whether you realize it or not, there is something built in to each of us that really wants to be recognized as special. And, why not? Think about it for a second. There are approximately 6 billion people on this planet and not one is exactly alike.

Even our children are vying for our attention to be recognized in their sports, academics or music involvement. It seems that we will always silently cry out to hear that we're OK and hope to have a stamp of approval. Each one of us is looking to show how different we are and how we can use our talents to contribute to this crazy world we live in.

If you're not sure that I'm accurate on this "being recognized" thing, let me ask a question:

What do you think makes a career or business grow and prosper? Corporate America has figured out that any successful business is dependent upon recognition.

That's why the word, "branding", has taken such a surge as being the key for more business. It seems all you hear about from marketing experts is the development of a brand. Why? Because it works! It's all about recognition, from the actual logo design they hope to burn into your data brain to the jingle or slogan that you wake up singing or thinking about.

The same is true in the job market. Everyone who has applied for a job hopes to do or say something in that interview that will make him or her stand apart from the others. One of the greatest forms of recognition is getting hired.

Make an effort the next few days to make a difference in someone's life by giving them some recognition for being an outstanding human. It's a good idea to start with your family first!

SuperQuickReminders ™

*Recognizing the good in those around you
only requires 2 simple actions.
Open your eyes and pay attention!*

*Everyone has negative and positive things
in their life.
Focusing on the positive sometimes
helps remove the negative.*

SuperQuickRecommendations ™

25 Ways To Win With People
How To Make Others Feel Like A Million Bucks
Bestselling Book by John C. Maxwell
Buy It...www.superquicklessons.com/winpeople

Be A People Person
Bestselling Book by John C. Maxwell
Buy It...www.superquicklessons.com/peopleperson

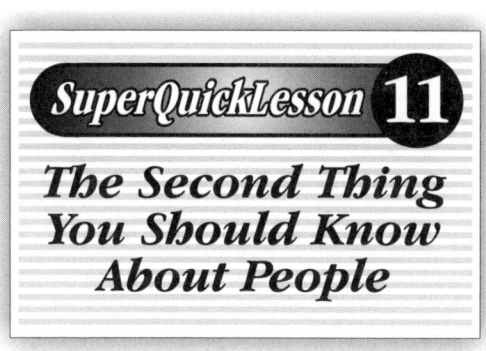

The second thing you should know about people is, *"Most People Love to be **Rewarded**."*

I have met very few people who can continue to produce for a long period of time for the sake of the cause only.

Surely by now you've heard the abbreviation W.I.I.F.M. which stands for "What's In It For Me?"

Unfortunately, this particular mentality can have its excesses and that's when you begin to see the "looking out for No. 1" attitude, instead of the overall good of the organization.

The most fulfilled people I have met, have figured out the balance between feeling good about accomplishing a job well done and the occasional need for reward.

One thing I hope everyone understands is that rewards are supposed to be good things. You know it's a reward because you feel better after you received it than before you received it.

It's the difference, let's say, between an unexpected bonus for going beyond the call of duty and a so-called promotion and maybe a raise which includes 10 times the responsibilities or hours you previously had.

However, I have come to realize that a reward for one person may not necessarily be a reward for someone else. For instance, some people prefer extra time off in comparison to a financial reward. For some reason I was always swayed by the word, "cash."

One day back in the '80's, at my first real employment as a commercial screen printer, I was afforded a surprise that I've never forgotten. It was Friday and the owner of the company came back and let us know that a particular job needed to be done that evening because the client was coming to pick it up first thing Monday morning. What he was asking for was volunteers. Not one employee raised their hand. I remember the war going on inside my head because I had a date with a special young lady from a nearby town. Slowly, I felt my arm raising and I said I would stay.

As I began the job, I'm sure the managerial staff was curious as to how I was amassing so much incredible speed in this particular assignment. I'll bet the thought came to them, "Wow! what would happen if he worked like this everyday?"

I'll never forget finishing the job, and as I was cleaning up, the owner came back and said, "Randy, I really appreciate you staying and I've heard that you are seeing a little girl from Sand Springs. Here's something that should get you a couple of hamburgers and a movie." Smiling, I took the folded check and put it in my pocket telling him, "thank you."

I was so focused on getting out of there I did not even look at the check until the owner's son came over to me a few minutes later. He mentioned how he saw his dad give me something and was curious about what it was. I pulled the check out of my pocket and was in shock that it was made out for $50. You need to realize that in the early '80's, a $50 check bought several hamburgers and a couple of movies for two. He was as surprised as I was. I'll never forget what he said, "Man, that's unbelievable! I have never known dad to give a bonus check!"

Now it's one thing to get a reward like everybody else, but there's an indescribable feeling that comes from a one-of-a-kind reward. It was that day, I decided to make it a habit to always go the extra mile. I came to the conclusion, that for some reason, the road to the extra mile was never crowded.

Now, I get a thrill from being on the other side of the reward system. There's not a feeling that compares to handing a bonus check or giving someone a "paid" day off when they least expect it.

The first quarter of 2005 afforded me the biggest opportunity to reward my team for breaking every sales and production record in the 20 plus year history of my company.

I'll never forget having them come into my office individually and presenting each of them with a check. I wanted to see their facial expressions after they took a look into their envelope. I had every display of emotion that has ever been available from hysterical laughter to sobbing. It's been said that it's better to give than it is to receive. I believe it.

SuperQuickReminders™

*People don't care how much you know,
until they know how much you care!*

*Some surveys have shown that money
isn't always the biggest motivator.
It's obvious that most people I know
didn't participate in that survey!*

Money (Still) Talks!

SuperQuickRecommendations™

Developing The Leader Within You
Bestselling book by John C. Maxwell
Buy It...www.superquicklessons.com/leaderyou

Developing The Leaders Around You
Bestselling book by John C. Maxwell
Buy It...www.superquicklessons.com/aroundyou

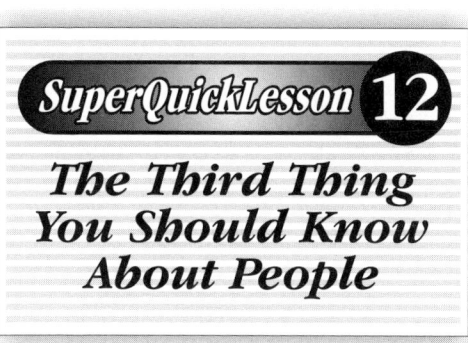

The Third Thing You Should Know About People

Try and never forget this third thing I've learned about people: *"Most People Love to be **Remembered**."*

Over the last 15 years, one skill I have tried to perfect probably more than any other, is the ability to remember names. I have seen more response and even displays of emotion from this one little skill than any other. There is something about the mention of our name that brings significance to our existence on this planet.

Do you remember how it felt to go into a restaurant or retail store and the manager or salesperson called you by name? You're first thought was probably, "Wow, I didn't even think they noticed me."

There is a distinct link between mentioning a name with showing that you care. Why? Your name is personal. It belongs to you. Yes, there may be millions of Marys, Johns, and the next generations of Joshs and Ashleys, but there is not one exactly alike.

That's why, in a crowd of people, when you hear your name called, you immediately turn around and think to yourself, "I wonder if they're talking to me?"

One of my goals is to try and remember everyone I meet by their first name. Here's a tip, the first name usually does it. Trying to always get that last name usually leads to my brain locking up.

Several years ago, I made the decision to get to know the first names of all the people that visited my local church. It is difficult to describe the impact it still has even today.

One particular young woman came with her aunt. In a quick visit after her aunt introduced her to me, it was apparent that she was trying to find her purpose in this world with decisions about school and a future career.

I will never forget, it was about six months later that she came to visit her aunt again. When I saw her come in, I immediately remembered her name. (It was easy because she shared my mother's name). As she walked by, I said, "Hi, Sherry, how have you been doing?"

No one around me expected her response. She broke down and began to cry and said these words that will stay with me forever, "I can't believe you remembered my name." Needless to say, that morning I found the power in remembering a name.

It's interesting to see when I'm attending a business function and I'm fortunate to remember a few names that it seems that those people you remember sort of gravitate to you. Don't wonder why. It's all in a name!

SuperQuickReminders ™

*There is a definite connection between
a persons name and their smile muscles.*

*When it's your turn in the check out line,
call the cashier by the name on their badge.
They'll probably treat you like a good friend!*

*Make a habit of remembering names.
The continuing exercise will build
strong relationships.*

SuperQuickRecommendations ™

Gung Ho!
Turn On The People In Any Organization
#1 Bestselling book by
Ken Blanchard & Sheldon Bowles
Buy It...www.superquicklessons.com/gungho

Zapp!
The Lightning Of Empowerment
Bestselling book by William C. Byham
Buy It...www.superquicklessons.com/zapp

Randy's
SuperQuickLessons - Skill #4 ™

Customer Service

SuperQuickLesson 13

Can I Get Some Help Over Here?

We've all experienced it. Waiters and waitresses that act as if you're invisible, going to a department store and figuring out that it would be easier to find the "lost ark" than it is to find a sales clerk, or how about calling your favorite electronics store to listen to the melodious sound of eternal ringing? I have found that when some companies want to connect you with customer service, what they have overlooked is the one thing that determines whether or not they even have a customer service department.

True customer service has always depended on having a "customer servant" that can be reached without exerting a tremendous amount of effort and time.

Everyone has seen the American stereotype servant in the movies: nannies, butlers, maids and chauffeurs. Even though it's Hollywood, the characters exhibit a sense of pride in who they work for and quickly see to it that their employers' needs are met.

Can you imagine what your business could do if your employees or co-workers realized that customers were actually paying to have their needs taken care of?

Over the several years of being in business I have tried to develop the "customer servant mentality." I have learned to know my customers' needs as individuals, and not as a list of products they are interested in.

"Customer Servanthood" is all about being willing and ready to serve the very moment the phone rings or the customer walks through the front door.

After I graduated from high school, I had an opportunity to work at a local department store. I quickly became the manager of the art and school supplies department. As the summer was coming to a close, I had an idea about how to better serve the mothers that would be coming in to buy school supplies for the next school year. I went to all the local schools and asked for each grade level's list of supplies.

I placed a blanket order to adequately take care of the needs of those that would be shopping down my aisles. Since the lists were almost identical, I stocked the shelves in the order they appeared on the lists.

My department was just to the right of the front door and I was able to pick out those who were coming to see me because they usually had the list in their hand. The enjoyable thing was when mothers came in and looked a little hurried or over-whelmed. I just calmly took the basket went over the list with them and told them the basket would be at the counter when they were ready to check out.

The store manager let me know numerous times how those

mothers couldn't believe how well I'd taken care of them.

Here are a few questions to help you get a pulse on your customer service activities.

1. Do you care "HOW" your customer receives what is needed from you or your company?

2. Do you have the answers to questions that might be asked about your service or products? Can you give intelligent recommendations?

3. Do you use voice mail more than necessary to inadvertently delay service to your customer?

4. Are you known for returning messages in minutes, hours, or days?

5. Do you fuel the fire of unsatisfied customers by your attitude, or do you help them focus on the issue of serving them to right any wrong?

6. When a problem arises regarding an order that appears to be out of your control, do you call the customer and give the status, or an explanation and a possible concession?

7. If you absolutely cannot get what the customer needs, do you have a network that can?

If you are indifferent to the first question, the rest of them won't even matter because it really boils down to an attitude of caring.

SuperQuickReminders ™

Customer Servant = Customer Service

The more creative you get taking care of customers, the more they tell their friends & some will just show up to see if it's true!

Do you realize that you may not be the only company that offers what you offer?

SuperQuickRecommendations ™

Raving Fans
#1 Bestselling book by
Ken Blanchard & Sheldon Bowles
Buy It...www.superquicklessons.com/raving

Customer Mania!
It's Never Too Late to
Build a Customer-Focused Company
book by Ken Blanchard, Jim Ballard & Fred Finch
Buy It...www.superquicklessons.com/mania

Recently, I was inspired to take a look at my customer service philosophy. It seems that most of my inspiration comes from experiences that keep me wondering how some companies stay in business.

A few months back I was hosting the monthly Breakfast Network for the Tulsa Chamber. That morning our guest speaker was, as I call her, the "Queen of Customer Service", Myra Golden. One of the questions opened for discussion at the tables was, "Is the customer always right?"

Now take a minute to think about that question because every time I hear it, I immediately know that if the question has to be asked it's because something went wrong. When you try to sort out what went wrong, the ultimate thing you will have to deal with is, who is at fault, in the mind of the customer?

Most mistakes are made because of poor communication. I frequently remind my production team of the importance of proper and effective communication. Things like taking good notes, asking for follow-up or confirmation e-mails or faxes. I've endeavored to train them that if they are ever brought to the

"Customer Courthouse" they had better have a convincing defense. In all honesty, most of the time when something goes wrong, it's usually our fault, and when that happens, all I care about is having the opportunity to make it right, to the point that our clients are glad we made the mistake.

Unfortunately, I have come to find out that many companies don't have the same, "Cost is No Object" fix-it policy as we do. Hopefully, when you or your team, make a mistake, you don't respond like the following:

When we changed the name of our safety sign company from The Randy Clay Company to U.S. SafetySign & Decal, it was time to get new business cards. I ordered a set for the young woman who runs my company and myself. I wanted the cards exactly the way one of our previous cards had been done and I communicated the exact layout with hopefully no room for misunderstanding. I even saw the proof and it looked as good as a jpeg file could look. A few days later, the cards arrived and didn't look like the original design. I simply wanted them re-done, and a few days later I received two new boxes. This time there was a box for me and a box for a totally different person on my staff that we hadn't ordered new cards for, and besides that, the e-mail address on her cards was wrong. The surprising thing was that they charged me for both sets. I perceived the attitude that it wasn't their fault. I'd done business with this company for a while and found it a little interesting that they weren't going to take responsibility for the first set of unsatisfactory cards. They acted as if we'd never discussed the cards expected layout and apparently the cards overall design was a matter of artistic opinion. Even though I went ahead and paid for both sets of cards I can promise it will end up costing them many times more in lost business than what it cost me for two boxes of business cards. My question is simply this, How long can a company stay in business if they disappoint a customer with the "it isn't our fault" attitude? Especially, when the evidence is clear. Whether you realize it or not, your competitors are waiting for you to develop such an attitude, and believe me, that when they see, hear or even smell it, they are merciless. One of my customers summed it up for me when he said to me, "Randy, everybody makes mistakes, but it's the way you take care of them that will keep them coming back to your company."

SuperQuickReminders ™

Success in business is largely determined
by how you can serve the customer
better than your competition does.

When serving customers, nobody's perfect.
It's whether or not you're able to erase
the imperfection from their minds that matters.

A servant is simply someone that takes care
of the needs of another.

SuperQuickRecommendations ™

Beyond WOW!
book by Myra Golden
& Dr. Jeffrey Magee
Buy It...www.superquicklessons.com/wow

10 SuperQuick Commandments
of Customer Service
(QuickRead E-Book)
by Randy Clay
Buy It...www.superquicklessons.com/10comm

SuperQuickLesson 15

Defusing The Disgusted!

Correct me if I'm wrong, but I have found only one business where the actual customer doesn't care one iota what kind of service he or she is receiving, and, since most of us aren't in the funeral business, there will come a day, sooner or later, when you will encounter a living, breathing (often heavily breathing), un-happy customer.

I can count on one hand how many irate customers I've had to deal with in all my years of being in business and my memory only recalls two.

The number one irate and totally disgusted customer of all time totally blew us away when we got the call. It was a specialty packaging company that we produced identification labels for. This particular label was mistakenly produced from an outdated print.

Man, was she steamed! "How could you all do this, I don't understand? We've never had this problem before what is the problem with your company?" She was so upset, my team asked me to take over negotiations. Believe me when I have to take over, "Houston we have a problem."

Give me a moment to describe this job. It was a small label about 1 and a half inches by 3 inches. They usually only order a few hundred a year. It has a single color imprint of a logo on it and the total order was a whopping 100 labels.

It's never been a big ticket order. I was really shocked by her reactions because she never asked what we would do about it, she just kept yelling that she didn't understand how we could make a mistake like this. All of a sudden, she's got me wondering how we could make such a horrible mistake.

After calming her down and imagining that someone in her production facility must have had a gun to her head, I told her I would personally be over with a new set of labels within an hour.

I told the team to double the order and bring them to my office. Thirty minutes later, I'm off to Ms. Unbelievable's production facility.

I walked in the door and she let me have it again. I didn't say a word. Finally she stopped yelling, I guess to take a breath and it looked to me like she was expecting an explanation. I handed her the package of labels and said " I really want to apologize for the mistake and to show how concerned we are about the trouble we've caused, we've doubled the order for you. She was speechless and it's a good thing, because I wasn't finished. I continued, "I think I know what caused the trouble and I sure could use your help. The next time that you are taking applications for new employees, would you mind forwarding the ones you've identified as "perfect" that you don't have an immediate position for? Because in all my years of hiring I haven't been able to find one perfect employee. I honestly believe that is why we made the mistake. I hope you'll accept our apology".

She closed her eyes and smiled and said, "as a matter of fact we don't have any perfect employees here either." Point given, point taken.

I found out about the second disgusted customer when I received a phone call letting me know that on an Internet bulletin board someone had posted a comment that they were "very unhappy" about a product they had purchased from us.

We've all heard the stats on how many people can find out about your shortcomings when someone didn't get what they expected. The Internet has now taken that to an unbelievable level.

First, I tried to e-mail the dissatisfied party and guess what? The e-mail address wasn't working. After spending a few days trying to figure out who it was so that I could get him or her back into "happy-land," I finally realized I had to post my own note in hopes of calming the rest of the potential customers within the association.

I knew from the bulletin that there wasn't going to be an opportunity to fix the oversight, so my plan was simple. In most cases, nothing calms the irritated customer quicker than a full, no strings attached R-E-F-U-N-D!

In my response, I asked the mystery customer if he had tried to contact us about the problem, emphasizing that the most important thing to us now was to totally refund any investment, including freight, if we just knew where to send it. I even thanked the customer for allowing us the opportunity to provide the product in the first place. I also put a side note to anyone else that had problems to call my 1-800 number and we would fix it immediately.

A couple of days later, I received another phone call that said, "Have you seen the bulletin board? It's turned into a Randy Clay Lovefest!"

Sure enough, a couple of extremely satisfied customers had posted comments about how well we'd taken care of them and that we were the best supplier they'd ever dealt with. Finally, the "Cheers" beat the "Jeers" 2-to-1.

By the way, I thought you'd like to know--the unhappy publisher never did call for that refund.

SuperQuickReminders™

If you think a refund is costly, you should have a closer look at the cost of lost business!

Everybody has a bad day now and then, just make sure yours isn't the same day as an disgusted customer!

They'll calm down once they see how you are going to take care of the problem. The goal is to make them glad you made the mistake.

SuperQuickRecommendations™

The Ultimate Customer Recovery Guidebook: How to Keep Customers Coming Back After a Service Mishap
E-book by Myra Golden
Buy It...www.superquicklessons.com/comeback

Selecting a Customer Relationship Management System for Total Complaint Management, Customer Win Back, &
How to Develop a Service Recovery Plan
E-booklets by Myra Golden
Buy It...www.superquicklessons.com/golden

SuperQuickLesson 16

No Reward For The Outlaw Employee

In the beginning of the 20th century, history tells us about a cub reporter that was given the mission of a lifetime. Andrew Carnegie, the early century steel giant, commissioned this young writer to devote twenty years of his life to researching and interviewing the most prestigious, respected and wealthiest men in the world of industry.

The goal of this writer was to document the philosophy behind these men's successes. One of the keys that these businessmen saw as mandatory to achieve financial success is surprisingly overlooked today. This key is also referred to as an actual law and I'm thankful that I learned to apply it when I entered the working world. It has definitely been one of the reasons that I have made it this far in my business career. It's called the "Law of Increasing Returns."

One of the things over the years I have come to quickly identify is the attitude that basically says, "I'm not going to do anything more than I have to do in order to get a paycheck."

After a while I found that a paycheck all of a sudden isn't big enough anymore, and some people begin to think that they should make more money just because they've been around a long time. With all the layoffs and downsizing we have seen, I hope people are starting to see that just because you show up doesn't necessarily mean you're worth keeping.

A few years ago I had the opportunity to share with a group about customer service and work ethic using a subject that some people don't understand, called, "Doing More Than Paid For."

I take the time to explain that if you are an employee of a corporation you basically have 2 sets of customers. Those who spend money on your product or service which come from outside the company but you also have those who are over you such as managers or supervisors. Taking care of the second group probably has just as much to do with your financial success as taking care of the first set of customers.

A few weeks later a young man that was in the audience came up to me and told me that my stories inspired him to change his attitude toward work and the way he approached each day.

He began to arrive at his place of employment thirty minutes early every day and started working before everyone else showed up. He did it with an attitude that it didn't matter whether he was ever paid for it or not. Two weeks later, his employer gave him a surprise raise.

The next time I saw him I asked him if he was still doing what he had started and, to my disappointment, he said "no."

When I asked why, he said that he buckled under the persecution and name calling of the other employees.

They were making references to the color of his nose and telling him that he was making them look bad. I almost lost my mind!

"That is exactly what I said would happen when I was challenging you to go the extra mile," I reminded him. I asked him who he was there to please? Hadn't his employer responded appropriately by giving him a raise?

The next time someone tells you that you are making them look bad, it should be obvious that they don't need any assistance from you. I'll bet they are doing a great job on their own!

Employees that have the "just do enough to get by" attitude will one day wonder why they aren't getting by!

The oldest version of the "Law of Increasing Returns" is the "Law of Seedtime and Harvest." Think about it ... have you ever just planted one seed and only gotten one seed back? Of course not, because we'd all starve to death! The same is true in the workplace, if you give a little more than is expected, then sooner or later it's going to come back in the form of something you need. It's a law of nature!

If you understand this law, you will realize the only thing that gives you the right to ask for more money, benefits, etc., is the fact that you have earned them in advance. You wouldn't ever be upset with your garden if it didn't produce something you didn't plant in advance, would you? Here's a thought ... when it comes to a possible layoff, who should they let go first? An *asset* or the *liability*?

Randy's SuperQuickReminders™

If you're not rendering more
service than you're being paid for,
Then you may be stuck only
being paid for what you are rendering.

One of the Laws of Nature
proves that you give first and get later.
That's probably why very few places
of employment pay in advance.

Randy's SuperQuickRecommendations™

Think and Grow Rich
Classic book by Napoleon Hill
Buy It...www.superquicklessons.com/thinkrich

The Law of Success in Sixteen Lessons
book by Napoleon Hill
Buy It...www.superquicklessons.com/successlaw

The Science of Personal Achievement
audio series by Napoleon Hill
Buy It...www.superquicklessons.com/science

Randy's
SuperQuickLessons - Skill #5 ™

Marketing

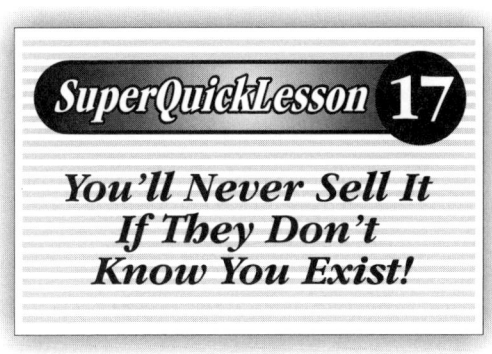

There is one thing that I can barely stand hearing a new or potential customer say when they call or come to my facility. It's the words, "We didn't even know you were here." Now, who's fault is that? I came to realize it wasn't their fault they didn't know I existed, it was mine. My simple definition for marketing is, using the best way possible to figure out what people want and then using the best way possible to let them know you're on the planet.

The first book I ever read on marketing was given to me from a local university professor. The title was *22 Immutable Laws of Marketing* with a subtitle that read *Violate Them at Your Own Risk*. It is my type of book, only 140 pages that are short sweet and to the point.

The first 2 laws basically re-programmed my philosophy about marketing my business.

The first law is, *The Law of Leadership - It's better to be first than it is to be better.*

The authors demonstrated the law of leadership by asking 2 questions.

1. What's the name of the **first** person to fly the Atlantic Ocean Solo? Charles Lindbergh, Right?

2. What's the name of the **second** person to fly the Atlantic Ocean Solo?

I had no idea. According to history his name is Bert Hinkler. They say that Hinkler was not only a better pilot than Lindbergh but his flight took less time and consumed less fuel.

The comparison to business was that most people go into business to compete not to dominate. Unfortunately, the majority of small businesses are destined to the arena of competition.

When I finally found my niche in 1988, I realized I wasn't the only manufacturer of safetysigns in the world. I also came to the realization that the leaders of the safetysign race had a 100 year head start.

Getting into my niche market was really a stroke of divine intervention.

I had originally started my screenprinting business to print radio station bumper stickers. Big quantities, with advertising on the back that paid for the printing, what a deal!

Unfortunately, I was late getting into that market also. Every time I thought I had a customer they started playing the "nickel game". Here's how it's played. Let's say I would submit a quote to print 20,000 bumper stickers at .075 cents each. The potential radio station would say, "Wow that sounds great! Give us a couple of days and we'll fax over a purchase order." Instead of receiving a purchase order I received a phone call that started out with, "We found a company that will do the order for .07 cents each, can you do them for .065 cents each? After a couple of years of playing that game, I was worn out and nearly broke.

One day in the midst of market dreaming a man with the title of Safety Director came in to my shop. He worked for a major oil drilling company in his hand was a 10" by14" metal sign.

He asked me if I could print him a few of the same design and layout on self- sticking vinyl. (That's the technical name for bumper sticker material)
I answered, "Sure how many do you need?"
"Just a few dozen to start with", he said.

That day was the start, of not only a great friendship, but a love for an industry that has taken very good care of me.

Like most small businesses I didn't have the financial resources to do major market research to find all the demographics of potential buyers and the other high tech information gathering.

I simply made the assumption that if one safety director was looking for a great company to make safetysigns for their drilling operations, there had to be other companies that had the same needs but didn't know I was even in existence.

I still have that metal sign in my office to remind me that you never know where the next big opportunity is going to come from. The first one was easy because he fortunately found me, but in order to break into an industry, I found out that I had to go gather in the rest of them.

SuperQuickReminders™

Marketing is a lot like fishing.
Your bait has a lot to do with your success!

Longevity in business has more to do with
finding a market first and then supplying
the needs of that market.

Just because you are in love with the product
you developed doesn't neccessarily mean
everyone else will be.

SuperQuickRecommendations™

The 22 Immutable Laws of Marketing
Violate Them at Your Own Risk
Bestselling book by Al Ries & Jack Trout
Buy It...www.superquicklessons.com/immutable

Getting Everything You
Can Out of All You've Got
book by Jay Abraham
Buy It...www.superquicklessons.com/jay

SuperQuickLesson 18

Getting Them To Come To You!

After reading the first law in the book, *22 Immutable Laws of Marketing* I was a little discouraged because I knew that I wasn't the second or third to enter the safetysign manufacturing arena, I was probably number 1,000,001.

That's why I was so thrilled to learn the second law which reads, *"The Law of Category - If you can't be first in a category, set up a new category to be first in."*

The authors then ask, what's the name of the third person to fly the Atlantic Ocean solo? If you didn't know that Bert Hinkler was the second person to successfully cross the Atlantic what are your chances that you'd know the third?

But if you're like me you have heard of the third person but you didn't know it. It's Amelia Earhart. Now here's the question. Is Amelia the third person to cross the Atlantic or the *first woman* to cross the Atlantic?

Throughout the chapter, the authors show mega successful businesses that found a category to be "first in" even though the product had already been on the market for years before they showed up.

The chapter gave excellent illustrations of companies that found new categories to dominate.

By now, everyone should know that DELL is not the first company to produce personal computers. However, DELL does dominate the category of personal computers ordered by phone.

Charles Schwab didn't open a better brokerage firm, he opened the first discount brokerage firm.

One point the book brings out is that people aren't usually interested in what's better, they flock to what's "new"!

My first marketing campaign was an inspiration from one of my favorite John Wayne movies.

I had just started researching my potential in the oil drilling industry and I noticed in the weekly TV Guide that next Saturday afternoon, "Hellfighters", with John Wayne was going to be on. In case you haven't seen it, the movie is about the oil well firefighter legend, Red Adair.

I had seen the movie several times over the years but this time I noticed that every vehicle in the film from the company airplane to John Wayne's Lincoln Continental, had a screenprinted decal stuck on the doors.

I'll never forget saying to myself, "wouldn't it be great to get a oil well firefighting company as a client?"

The next Monday I made a call to my safety director friend who had by this time been transferred to Houston, Texas. I asked him if he had to work with any oil well firefighter companies. Believe it or not, one such company had an equipment yard next to his. One phone call and 8 months later we had produced the most elaborate and gorgeous sticker the oil industry had ever seen, Neal Adams - Firefighting and Blowout Specialists. Six different colors on a gold chrome background.

My plan was to print a bunch of extra stickers to use as samples. One thing I learned about the industry is that hard hat stickers are the items of desire. Almost everyone collects them and if a new one comes out everybody goes crazy trying to find the source.

Being that the wild well control business seemed exciting and glamorous every company seemed to compete as to who could have the best logo and sticker design. I decided to leverage my company into the hype.

The first marketing plan involved a DBA name that the industry would see as a connection to the oil industry. We called it Wild Ink Control - SafetySign and Decal Specialists. The logo I designed was worthy to be compared to the ones in the fire fighting business. I'll never forget that first industry convention we went to in Houston. We had black coveralls with our multicolor logo embroidered on the back and hats to match. We had people come by thinking we were another fire fighting company.

One thing I teach about trade show marketing is, if an attendee hesitates, they're mine. You've got to have something visual that makes them stop, even if it's just a second. We invited them to fill out a very short 4 question survey for a chance to win one of our hats. We also gave them a hard hat sticker for spending time with us. Even today I create give-a-ways based on what I've learned that people hang on to the longest.

Remember that people gravitate to what's new and we were definitely new. Until we showed up no one had taken such a flashy approach to get the attention of the drilling industries safety directors, like we did.

I did realize that most of what we were doing was just a fad. Just because you're bringing something new and exciting doesn't necessarily mean you're going to be around a long time. Most industries are looking for longevity from their vendors.

Even though I still get mail addressed to Wild Ink Control, it was just a fad that some of the older guys remind me of. Some of them still have the hats setting in their offices after all these years.

The thing we took first place in was how we figured out what every safety director needs. It was a pain free way to order safetysigns. Even today, most safety directors will buy signs from catalogs. When a new potential client asks for a catalog my staff and I answer, "Don't you have enough catalogs?" I came up with way to service the client without the need of a catalog.

Picture this, you need 100 different signs for your oil or gas company. How long do you think it would take to find all 100 in a catalog and actually record the sign number and place the order? We found out it can take days, especially if you are looking for a sign that isn't in the book in the first place. How do you know it's not in there without looking? You don't.

That's why the next evolution of my company name was U.S. SafetySign & Decal - At Last, Freedom From the Catalog!

How we do it is classified common sense!

SuperQuickReminders™

*The easier it is to do business with
your company, the easier it is to find
new business!*

*Always remember the 3 ways
to grow a business.*
1. Get more customers (duh)
2. Get customers to buy more stuff.
3. Get customers to buy more often.

SuperQuickRecommendations™

Randy's First Run of Publicity!

**Article in the Tulsa World Newspaper
Front page of the Business Section**

Good Sign *Movie Inspired Screen Printer
Written by Ray Tuttle*

Read the article at...
www.superquicklessons.com/goodsign

SuperQuickLesson 19

Outrageous Is Contagious!

I was at my desk when the mail came and within a few minutes my assistant brought in my batch of junk mail. For several days I had been thinking about my next area of focus concerning marketing. I had tried different types of advertising but in some cases never saw even a copper penny of return on the investment.

As I was going through different ads in the mail, one particular ad caught my attention. It was a brochure in the form of a mini-book from the nation's largest producer of self-help information. It was introducing a 12 cassette tape series titled, *The Power of Outrageous Marketing - - -Using the 10 Time-Tested Secrets of Titans, Tycoons, And Billionaires to get Rich in your Own Business.* The brochure included a no-cost, no-obligation, 30 day free trial. Within a few days that series was in my hot little hands and plugged into my cassette player.

The thing that intrigued me the most was the authors focus on publicity whenever possible. One comment that has always stuck with me was, "get all the publicity you can for as long as you can." I noticed that the author also placed a lot of emphasis on writing. One particular part of the series and probably my favorite, was titled, *How to Live Forever: Establish Yourself as an Immortal by Writing a Book.* He shared how to write one in 6 days. He also shared about the importance of public speaking as a way to market your business. It wasn't until years later that the opportunity to use these time-tested secrets came into my life.

One day, I was browsing at one of the independent bookstores in Tulsa. I believe the reason that this store has lived through the invasion of discount bookstores is because of the massive list of magazine titles that they carry. I picked up a magazine that I had never noticed before called the *Oklahoma Business Monthly*. As I was flipping the pages I noticed an article about one of my clients. The article was a historical account of different successful business people that started their companies in Oklahoma. This article was about the founder of an oil drilling company that I had been supplying product to for years. I loved the story.

Knowing that they probably didn't print all the information they gained from the research I called the publisher and asked to speak to the author of the article. They connected me with the editor and she began to inquire as to why I needed to talk to the author. After a brief explanation and a quick history of my company, she asked if I would be interested in participating in an article they featured every month called Entrepreneur Q&A? What they did was send a list of questions with the hope that the answers would help other business people. Of course the answers were subject to an editorial review and approval. When I received the questions, somehow I knew this was going to be the beginning of my journey in publicity.

I e-mailed all the questions back the next day and waited. A little over a week later, I received a phone call that my responses were going to be published and they wanted to make an appointment for their photographer to come by. I had seen the type of pictures that they had taken for other companies that had participated in the same article, and believe me they were boring!

I had a different plan in mind for my picture. I asked if the photographer could please come by and visit without a camera. I admit, I am not anything to look at, so my joke was that I didn't want to be responsible for her equipment failure on our first visit.

The day she came by started with introductions and my usual 20 questions about her. Finally, I asked her if she had reviewed my article and she said, "yes". I then unveiled my plan to have a picture that included everything I had discussed in the article, in the photograph. She got really enthusiastic and let me know that she had been hoping to shoot something a little more exciting than some of her previous sessions. I showed her my ideas of the set and set up the time for the shoot. She did a fantastic job and after the article was published we received several comments as to how "cool" it was to actually see the things I talked about. To read the article and view the picture, go to *www.superquicklessons.com/entq&a* .

Thinking ahead, I knew that not long after the magazine had been distributed it would sooner or later wind up in the ol' trash can. I was again reminded of one of the phrases from the outrageous marketing tape series that said, "get all the publicity you can for as long as you can." But how was I going to keep this going?

I decided to become a columnist, but what would I need to do to convince them to let me start writing for their magazine. I had "NO" writing experience. One thing I share with young business people is, that the success of most objectives is 80% presentation. I knew this was going to be a one shot opportunity and the presentation better be a good one.

I called the editor and said , "I want to show you and your staff how much I appreciate you publishing my article. I want all of you to join me for lunch." (I suggested a particular restaurant and because it was such a nice one, I knew that they'd jump at a chance to go there.) I also mentioned that if they joined me I would make sure that everyone in the restaurant would have a copy of the current issue of the magazine the day we went to lunch. (How's that for bait?) She sounded skeptical about the magazine stunt but asked if the owner of the publishing company could join us? I responded with, "of course, just pick the day". They got back with me on a date that would work for their staff.

Being that I knew the owner of the restaurant I had to make another presentation to him. I shared with him what I wanted to pull off and I would give away a few free meals during the lunch hour. He thought it was a great idea and we set the date.

When the day arrived I was ready. I had two lovely greeters at the front doors letting customers know that we were giving several free lunches for those who submitted a business card. Every place setting had a complimentary copy of the current issue of the *Oklahoma Business Monthly,* and of course, my article was in it.

I'll never forget the facial expressions of the publishing staff when they walked in the door and saw their magazines everywhere. We were seated at a huge round table in the center of the room, and after much conversation and a great lunch the owner asked me what I thought of the magazine. I told him I was impressed with the research that his staff had gathered in order to come up with interesting and pertinent articles to help the business person. Then I asked, "would you be open to reviewing an article submitted by a person that had actually been in business for several years?" He answered with, "that's a great suggestion". With that, I opened my briefcase and handed out a one page story about customer service to everyone at the table. The editor started laughing and said, "why am I not surprised?" The owner said this looks great, let us go over it and we'll get back to you."

The next week one of the staff called and said you won't believe this but a few weeks ago we had a magazine consultant teach us what we should be looking for when choosing articles for the magazine. Your article met all the criteria! How would you like to write for us every month?"

That was the day I became a columnist!

For over 2 years I wrote a column every month. The magazine eventually merged with another publication and I began to see the writing on the wall. My days were numbered, and that part of my writing adventure came to an end.

For the last couple of years I've been writing a weekly column for a local business journal.

However now I'm extremely excited about what I have been learning about what the internet has to offer in the marketing arena for those that have a knack for writing.

A couple of years ago I was listening to a tape series when the speaker made the comment that if you didn't have a presence on the world wide web by 2005 it was going to be very difficult for you to catch up when it comes to marketing your business.

Like it or not the internet is here to stay.

It wasn't until I went to a marketing conference in May of 2005 that I came to the realization that I had better start getting internet marketing savvy.

At that conference I finally met the "E-zine Queen" Alexandria Brown.

If you're not familiar with the term e-zine it's the short form of electronic magazine.

The idea of the e-zine is to develop a database of subscribers that are interested in your products or services. The e-zine helps you stay in touch in the fastest way possible. You can send one weekly, monthly or just when you have a special announce-ment. Some are published as plain text messages and other are published with more of a graphic design called "html".

The best e-zines have an article that instructs or inspires you to the next level of your business and then gives you updates of products or services.

Earlier in the year I had subscribed to the "Queen Ali's" e-zine called **Straight Shooter Marketing**. Her style is awesome she writes personally and professionally. Her weekly e-zine always has a featured article that will help you grow your business. She also lets you know what's going on in her life. From her stories, it's obvious that she's the ultimate California Girl.

One day, I just decided to give her office a call and was I surprised when she answered the phone. I had a few questions about her main product titled, **Boost Business with your Own E-zine.** I was pretty convinced that building a list of subscribers and communicating with them through an e-zine was the direction I wanted to go. I asked her a simple question, "Ali, if I do what you've done will I get the results you've gotten? She quickly answered, "absolutely"!

I don't know if you realize it, but it seems that information products are doubling every day. There are so many products out there, that it will actually take eternity to get through it all. That's why I look for experts in the fields I'm interested in. I check their track record and find out if what they are selling works. An e-zine is just one great way to get your business out there and I suggest you hurry and get on the wave.

For some reason, writing really does set you up as an expert and it seems that people love doing business with experts.

SuperQuickReminders ™

The success of most marketing campaigns
is 80% presentation.

After you find something that actually works,
then find the answer to...
"How can I keep this going?"

If you're going to model yourself
after someone, make sure they are
a successful someone.

SuperQuickRecommendations ™

The Power of Outrageous Marketing!
Using the 10 Time-Tested Secrets of Titans, Tycoons, And Billionaires
to get Rich in your Own Business.
Audio Program by Joe "Mr. Fire" Vitale
Buy it...www.superquicklessons.com/mrfire

Boost Business with Your Own E-zine
Study Course
by the "E-zine Queen" Alexandria Brown
Buy it...www.superquicklessons.com/ezinequeen

SuperQuickLesson 20

Take It To The Masses

Some very interesting things began to happen after I started writing. People thought that I was an authority on growing a business. Go figure. All I did was tell stories about the adventures I had experienced in the 20 years of starting and operating my small business.

One of my goals while writing for the **Oklahoma Business Monthly** was to get a cover story about the business books I had read that caused my business to grow.

My editor and I called it **Small Business 102--- A Top 10 List of Business Books Every Business Person Must Read.**

I offered a free book at the end of the article to anyone that would respond with a question or comment. I had talked to Harvey Mackay's assistant, Greg Bailey about donating a case of Harvey's book, **The Rolodex Network Builder**, which was strategically the last book I reviewed in my article.

(Let me quickly remind you of the reason I started writing in the first place. It was to be able to market my business.)

One of the first responses to my cover story was from the president of a company that manufactured industrial chemicals.

When I received his e-mail he wanted to know where to get the books I recommended in the article. The e-mail felt a little urgent because he was going overseas and wanted the books to take on his trip. I called and asked if I could bring him the books and he was really surprised that I offered. That same afternoon I was in his office discussing the books when he asked the question that I was hoping that a book delivery would produce. He asked,"What kind of business do you have?" I answered, "the name of my company is U.S. SafetySign & Decal. We manufacture safety signs for industrial compliance. Do you have a safety director?" With a push of a button he called his safety director to his office and introduced me to her. He instructed her to give me a tour and if they needed any safety signs for the current production facility or the expansion they were breaking ground for, he wanted to start buying from me. He didn't know me from Adam and all of a sudden I'm a new vendor just like that. It's amazing the credibility that writing can give you.

If you would like to view the list of the top 10 business books with my reviews go to *www.superquicklessons.com,* and sign up for my free e-zine and you'll automatically receive access to it.

The next interesting thing that happened was when one of the magazines editorial staff volunteered to serve on our local chamber of commerce's speakers committee. The chamber was presenting an annual business and technology trade show and they were looking for speakers to do "break out seminars" during the 2 day event. The magazine staffer let them know she had a guy that would do it. I thought, public speaking? Me? My mind went crazy about the potential marketing opportunities this event would afford.

I titled my presentation, *4 Things You Should Never Go To Work Without!* I couldn't believe the response and I don't think the chamber was able to believe it either.

After my presentation, a line of people formed, wanting to talk to me. The line grew to the entire length of the seminar area. I was blown away. I had to ask the crowd to follow me out into the showroom because there was supposed to be another presentation starting right after mine.

That was the day I became a business speaker!

To wrap up this lesson I want to let you know that of the 2 most common types of marketing, advertising and publicity, you need to understand that publicity is the gold mine for small business. Publicity gives you something you can't buy with advertising and that is credibility. To better get an understanding about the difference, you should read, *The Fall of Advertising and the Rise of PR* by Al and Laura Ries. (Al was the co-author of the book, *22 Immutable Laws of Marketing* that I mentioned earlier in this section.)

SuperQuickReminders™

Everybody has a book inside them, but most people leave this world without getting it printed!

Publicity and becoming a columnist or an author gives you something you can't buy, it's credibility.

One of the best assets for any career is the ability to make a presentation.

SuperQuickRecommendations™

Randy Clay's Small Business 102
SuperQuickReviews *of the*
Top 10 List of Business Books
Every Business Person Must Read.
Subscribe to **SuperQuickLessons E-Zine**
and receive reviews for **FREE**
www.superquicklessons.com

The Fall of Advertising and the Rise of PR .
Bestselling book by Al and Laura Ries
Buy It... www.superquicklessons.com/thefall

SuperQuickLesson BONUS

Michelangelo is Still Dead!

The thrill over the last couple of years has been the blending of my speaking opportunities with my business marketing. Think about it. Every introduction let's the audience know about my company.

I do realize that not everybody is going to become a public speaker but I do believe every one had better become extremely skillful at marketing on the internet if their business is going to continue to grow.

If you remember in one of the previous lessons, I mentioned going to a marketing seminar in May of 2005. I went with the desire to learn how to profitably market my first book, *Business Lessons with Sharkmaster, Jr.* (If you never got a copy of it don't worry, you are holding the new and improved version in your hands.)

What I learned was unbelievable. One platform speaker that caught my attention was Tom Antion. (pronounced an-tee-on). Besides being a great showman and speaker he is a genius on internet marketing. I purchased his program called *Electronic Marketing Butt Camp.* After listening to a few parts of the program I decided to call his office, and believe it or not, he answered the phone. After a few questions I talked him into letting me join his **Great Internet Marketing Mentoring Program**. Most people would choke at the contract but I have always said, "I don't care what it costs, if I can tell it's worth it."

The great thing about his program, unlike the other programs I looked at, was his accessibility. His program lasts for one year with a call every week. One thing he asked me to do was to quit thinking in terms of only one website, but to begin to think in terms of websites plural.

My first concern was, " how far behind am I?" He assured me that only about 3-4% of those doing business on the net are really making money, and that I had nothing to worry about.

He shredded my first website into unrecognizable pieces. It was a great art piece but had no ability to bring in traffic for product sales.

He mentioned that most web designers know more about graphic design than they do about making money using the net.

I shared with him a few adventures I had with web designers in the past. He was right that they do know a tremendous amount about design, and I've experienced that they even have a tendency to get their feelings hurt if you don't like or prefer their masterpiece. In one presentation meeting with a company I had hired to help me develop my first website one young designer told me I was too "picky". The young manager sat there and said nothing. Being that I was paying the bill, I informed them all that I had the privilege of being picky and asked if we were going to continue or should I go elsewhere?

I have a dozen stories of similar experiences that maybe I'll write about in the future.

The next thing Tom did was encourage me to put Sharkmaster, Jr. to bed, permanently. Actually we had a mercy killing. What we came up with, is what you're holding in your hands. *SuperQuickLessons* is a brand that we are developing that best describes what I'm about. I really don't get a lot of time to spend with people, so I have always desired to inspire and motivate with what time I've been given and do it in such a way that people will never forget it.

The point of this little lesson is, that it's time for you, if you haven't already, to start getting a little knowledge about how the internet can take your business to new levels. Always keep in mind that just because someone tells you they can design you a website, they may or may not be able to help you make money.

The primary purpose of the web for a business is to make money. Repeat that after me. *The primary purpose of the web, for a business, is to make money!*

It's not just a high dollar gallery for web designers to display their masterpieces.

This book you are holding is a result of having good mentors that have helped me develop a product that actually is marketable.

SuperQuickReminders™

After the web designer has shown you their portfolio, ask them to share how much money the site has made for their client.

Like it or not the web is here to stay. It might be to your best business interest to open a surf shop.

You don't have to know everything about the internet, you just have to find a teenager that does.

SuperQuickRecommendations™

The Ultimate Guide to Elelctronic Marketing for Small Business
Best Selling book by Tom Antion
Buy It...www.superquicklessons.com/ultimate

Butt Camp Elelctronic Marketing for Small Business
Audio Program by Tom Antion
Buy It...www.superquicklessons.com/buttcamp

The Great Internet Marketing Mentor Program
12 month Mentoring Program with Tom Antion
Buy It...www.superquicklessons.com/mentor

Clichés That Kill!

The person that came up with the old phrase, "Sticks and stones may break my bones, but words will never hurt me" was either hard-of-hearing or completely deaf.

The fact of the matter is that words are the most powerful things we possess in the shaping of our personal worlds and also the worlds of others.

I know that you've seen people that soared and excelled when given a positive affirmation and also people that felt belittled and even worthless at a non-constructive critical comment. It's amazing to me that some of the things that we say have little or no thought behind them because we've heard them so often we repeat them like a parrot. One thing about words we need to always remember is that they are supposed to paint pictures. For instance, when I say "cat" do you think C-A-T ... or do you picture an actual cat?

When I have the opportunity to share with people about this subject, I always emphasize the importance of speaking words that paint pictures of success instead of pictures of failure.

There are a few clichés I have learned to eliminate from my vocabulary over the years, like "What you don't know can't hurt you." I found out the opposite is more true, and some things you don't know can actually kill you! I've learned that there are certain things in business that if you don't know them, can destroy the business or continually stunt its growth.

The unfortunate thing that many don't realize is that the things we allow to come out of our mouths really do determine the level of success we see in our business and personal lives.

The good ol' boy that uses his mouth to continually criticize his boss and/or fellow employees, wife or "old lady," and his "never-gonna-amount-to-anything" kids, shouldn't be too disappointed when he becomes jobless, lonely and the father of a dysfunctional next generation.

The next cliché that really gets me is when I used to hear my UPS buddy leave and say, "Don't work too hard!" The reason that I know that phrase is just a non-thinking cliché is because I don't know one UPS delivery person that doesn't have the appearance of working hard. Years ago, I came up with my own cliché as an answer to that one. I simply say, "Thanks. I wish I could take that recommendation, but not today!" Please don't misunderstand. I do try to implement "the work smarter, not harder" process, but experience has shown me that both really work great together. However, I have seen some people take the "don't work too hard" thought too seriously.

The last cliché I want you to think about is one I can't stand! I have always been an employer that wants to know what ideas and thoughts someone on the team can bring to the planning table. My team learned years ago that the answer to my question, "What do you think?" should never be, "I try not to." For some people, it's obvious that this response may be true if you look at the mistakes they continue to make.

The expanded version of the above killer cliché is, "They don't pay me to think!" Now I would understand this coming from someone who always had his or her ideas put on the back burner, but the people that are fluent in this kind of communication often have the just-get-by mentality.

I want to challenge you to take an inventory of your vocabulary and speaking habits. Ask yourself if the things you are constantly saying are actually adding to your life or taking away from it.

If your work situation isn't what you'd like it to be, see if there is any adjustment you could make in the things you say about or to your employer or fellow employees. Do the same in your other relationships as well. I'll bet when you change the way you talk, you'll see a change in your quality of life.

Randy's

Once In A Life-time Opportunity...x2

Opportunity #1

Finally Meeting Harvey Mackay

I've had a number of people comment that they loved my story about finally meeting my long distance and literary mentor, Harvey Mackay.

As impossible as it seemed that I would ever meet him, I'm reminded that it doesn't matter how impossible your dreams seem to be, if you hang on to them long enough, you'll see the majority come true.

Every year starting in 1990, I called Harvey's assistant, Greg Bailey, to ask if Harvey was going to be anywhere near Tulsa, Oklahoma for a speaking engagement, and the answer was always, "not this year."

In January of 2000 you can imagine the shock when Greg said, "Randy, you're not going to believe it." Sure enough, he was coming to Tulsa on February 17 to speak. All I wanted to know was, "Who do I call?"

I finally made contact with the woman in charge of the reservations, and she informed me that she only had a few tickets left and she'd be glad to send me one.

Even though hearing him speak was next on my wish list, I

honestly didn't think I'd have a chance to actually meet him.

I arrived early to find my seat, and then I went on the hunt to find that nice woman that made this day possible. After finding her and giving my sincerest thanks, she asked the question that I had been waiting to hear for what seemed to be forever: "Would you like to meet him?"

My only regret was that I didn't bring a book for him to sign, but fortunately he was giving everyone a copy of his book, *The Harvey Mackay Rolodex Network Builder,* which I put in my pocket when I found my seat.

I'll never forget his first words after we were introduced: "You wrote me a letter, didn't you?"

With a puzzled look I answered, "Yes sir, I did." He then pointed at my lapel. I was wearing the shark pin he sent me when he wrote me back.

"I only sent those pins to the people that wrote me," he said, "and as a matter of fact, I personally answered over 300,000 letters." (I still wonder if I heard him right, but knowing him and how he operates I would never doubt it.)

He then asked, "Do you have all my books?"

I replied, "Yes sir, all in hardback."

"How about my tape series?"

"Yes sir."

"Even my latest one?"

"Are you talking about the one with the two bonus tapes? That was an excellent series," I said with a smile.

I then commented that the one thing I didn't have was his

autograph in one of his books.

I pulled the Rolodex book out of my coat pocket, which he gladly signed. "You don't have a copy of this book, do you?" he asked.

"As a matter of fact, I have 2 other ones," I answered proudly. I'll never forget his smile.

One of Harvey's famous sayings is: "Never say 'no' for the other guy." In other words, make a presentation and if you get rejected, *big deal,* because you'll never know the answer until you ask.

I had heard that the format of this particular meeting was one where they encouraged you to write a question on a 3-by-5 index card and they would randomly select a few for him to answer. Knowing the chances of him picking my card were leaning toward the impossible side, I prepared a 2 sided full-color card with a special request.

As we were finishing, I pulled the card out of my pocket. It had a shark bite out of the corner and it asked him to consider co-authoring a book with me in 2008 (the 20th anniversary of **Swim with the Sharks**).

He chuckled and said, "Randy I won't promise that I'll write a book with you, but I can probably help you get yours published."

As we were walking out, he turned to me and said, "I know one thing you don't have. Call my secretary and tell her to send you one of my 'Shark Ties' and get yourself a blue suit to wear with it." And that is exactly what I did!

Opportunity #2

One Whole Day with Harvey Mackay

One of my favorite events that the Tulsa Chamber of Commerce sponsors every year, in the month of August, is called, "Restaurant After Hours".

For the last couple of years, the event has been held at our local aquarium. It seems every restaurant in the city shows up for this little trade show.

At the 2004 event, another member of the chamber came up to me and said, "tell me how in the world did you get Harvey Mackay to come to Tulsa in October?"

Apparently my friend wasn't a master at reading facial expressions because mine was definitely saying, "I have no idea what you are talking about." A few minutes later, someone else congratulated me for bringing Harvey to Tulsa. I was confused.

The only thing I knew that Harvey had going on was the release of his new book, *We got Fired...and it was the best thing that ever happened to us.* Harvey's assistant Greg Bailey had graciously sent me a ring binder with a first revision rough draft, a few weeks prior.

I finally found the events coordinator for our chamber to ask if she knew anything about Harvey coming in October?

She proceeded to give me the scoop which was that Harvey was coming to speak at the luncheon during the Business & Technology Showcase in October. We were going to be his third stop in his 38 city book tour. The Tulsa World (our daily newspaper), and the chamber, had worked out a deal to get him to come.

Even though I had a million questions, the one that came to the surface was, "Who is introducing him at lunch? She got bright eyed and said, "I think it should be you!"

The next morning I called Harvey's assistant Greg Bailey and said, "Hi Greg this is Randy, 'chopped liver', Clay, tell me, is Harvey really coming to Tulsa as part of his book tour?"
"Oooh, Randy I'm sorry for not letting you know, but he sure is," he replied.
"Tell me Greg, who is going to be his escort while he's here?"
"His publicist in New York takes care of that for him. If you are interested, I'll give them your information and maybe they'll call you."
"Thanks Greg, and tell them I'll take great care of him."

Could it be possible? Would I get an opportunity to have a whole day with Harvey Mackay?

Weeks went by, and no call from the publicist. One bit of exciting news was that the newspaper had excitedly agreed to let me introduce him at lunch. What a privilege!

Then one day, I got a call from the chamber that asked if

I would like to come and see the new marketing campaign for the luncheon.

I couldn't get down to their office fast enough. After looking everything over, the chamber's marketing director mentioned she had talked to Harvey's publicist the day before and told him that the man introducing Harvey at the luncheon was a local author and businessman whose book Harvey had endorsed last year.

When I asked if she happened to have the name and number of the publicist handy, she went over to her desk and wrote it down for me.

One thing I learned a long time ago was that if you've got something to offer, it's not always the best to have someone else represent you. Nobody can sell you, like you!

I called the publicist, introduced myself and said I would like to apply for a job. He chuckled and asked what job I could want, being that I lived in Tulsa?

"Well, David, I'm applying for the position of Harvey's escort when he comes to Tulsa in October. Being that I was born and raised here, there is not one place he would need to go that I couldn't get him there in good fashion." By the way, I need to mention that my services will cost you nothing."

Randy, as a matter of fact we don't have a contact in Tulsa, I guess you're hired. I'll be sending you the details of his radio and television interview schedule in the next week or so.

I didn't realize that the information would come just a few days before his arrival, giving me just a little bit of time to plan the route for his different interviews. That day finally arrived and I was ready.

As I was waiting for Harvey's 4:00pm arrival, the young man in charge of directing the private jets to their parking places looked at me and said, "aren't you Randy Clay?" Looking a little surprised I said, "Yes, I am." Figuring that he saw my name on a contact list, he continued, "I heard you speak last year at the annual business banquet in the town I live in. I still remember what you talked on." He began reciting the part of my program that impressed him the most. Needless to say, we had a great visit and I was totally flattered.

Within a few minutes, the plane arrived and my young friend directed the jet to a stop and rolled out a small red carpet. One of the pilots came over to my vehicle and asked me to climb aboard. As I was approaching the door I heard Harvey yell, "is Randy here yet?" I yelled back, "I'm here Sharkmaster!"

"Get in here and help me with this stuff and grab that paper for me." I started chuckling because he had stuff everywhere and I mean everywhere. After we got everything collected we headed off to the hotel.

He wanted to freshen up for the reception the chamber had planned for the evening.

After getting everything up to his room he pulled a chair up right in front of the television, turned on CNN, and told me to sit down and let him know if anything interesting was happening in the pre-presidential election coverage. Harvey's prediction of the election outcome was based on the stock market of all things. I watched the stock market as election day approached, and Harvey's prediction was right on. Unbelievable.

While unpacking his clothes, he started looking a little worried that he was missing a black suit. I said, "Harvey is that it, under that pile of white shirts?" "Well it sure is... Oooooh would you look at this! Have you ever seen a suit so wrinkled? I told that guy at Neiman Marcus if the wrinkles don't come out, I'm bringing it back. This is the suit that I am wanting to wear to the luncheon."

I whipped out my cell phone and called a friend that owned a cleaners to see if she could have a suit pressed before tomorrow morning? No problem. "Harvey I can have the suit pressed and back up here in the morning." Looking a little impressed he said he wanted to try something first.

"Randy, here's a little trick that will serve you well in the future. It calls for, hot shower steam, 3 minutes hanging on the bathroom door and there you are, winkle free!

It really worked because he showed it to me excitedly saying, "do you remember how wrinkled this was? Well do ya?" "Harvey that's amazing." (as a matter of fact I've used that trick several times since and with the same success.)

After the reception we returned to the hotel and he asked me if I was an early riser?
"Yes sir."
"Great, call me at 4:45 in the morning and be here by five. I've got an interview at 6."

He had three interviews before 10 am and a couple more in his room before the luncheon. Between every one of them was a personal lesson on how to market a book. I will never forget that morning.

The luncheon was sold out and the crowd was over 800 in number. Everyone thought I'd be nervous about doing an introduction for such an icon in the business world. Me nervous? A little. Excited over such an opportunity? You bet!!!

I don't think that Harvey will ever forget the introduction a little Tulsa businessman gave him, and Tulsa will never forget the great speech he gave us.

The most memorable moment was when I was assisting Harvey as he was autographing his books, and when several people also had brought copies of my book that they wanted me to sign. So there I was, signing books right next to one of the greatest business authors in history and the only thing I regret is not having anyone to take a picture.

I'll never forget that autograph line, it was as long as the convention center, yet he spent a moment with every single person. Amazing? No, that's Harvey, and like I said in my introduction at lunch that's why, "he's my hero!"

International Bestsellers by Harvey Mackay

Swim with the Sharks Without Being Eaten Alive
*Buy It...*www.superquicklessons.com/harveyswim

Beware the Naked Man Who Offers You His Shirt
*Buy It...*www.superquicklessons.com/harveyshirt

Sharkproof
*Buy It...*www.superquicklessons.com/harveyproof

Dig Your Well Before You're Thirsty
*The **Only** Networking Book You'll Ever Need*
*Buy It...*www.superquicklessons.com/harveydig

Pushing the Envelope
All the Way to the Top
*Buy It...*www.superquicklessons.com/harveypush

NEW We Got Fired!
...And It's the Best Thing That Ever Happened To Us!
*Buy It...*www.superquicklessons.com/harveyfire

The Harvey Mackay Rolodex® Network Builder
*Buy It...*www.superquicklessons.com/harveyrolodex

Randy's SuperQuickRecommendations™

National Bestsellers by Blair Singer

SalesDogs
*Buy It...*www.superquicklessons.com/salesdogs

SalesDogs Training School
Audio program
*Buy It...*www.superquicklessons.com/dogtraining

NEW ## *The ABC's of Building a Business Team That Wins*
*Buy It...*www.superquicklessons.com/abc

National Bestsellers by Harry Beckwith

Selling the Invisible
*Buy It...*www.superquicklessons.com/harryselling

The Invisible Touch
*Buy It...*www.superquicklessons.com/harrytouch

What Clients Love: A Field Guide to Growing Your Business
(Compact Disc)
*Buy It...*www.superquicklessons.com/harrylove

Randy's SuperQuickRecommendations™

International Bestsellers by Ken Blanchard, Ph.D.

The One Minute Manager
*Buy It...*www.superquicklessons.com/oneminute

The Power Of Ethical Management
*Buy It...*www.superquicklessons.com/ethical

Raving Fans
*Buy It...*www.superquicklessons.com/raving

Customer Mania!
It's Never Too Late to
Build a Customer-Focused Company
*Buy It...*www.superquicklessons.com/mania

Gung Ho!
Turn On The People In Any Organization
*Buy It...*www.superquicklessons.com/gungho

International Bestsellers by Spencer Johnson, M.D.

The One Minute Salesperson
*Buy It...*www.superquicklessons.com/spencersales

Who Moved My Cheese?
*Buy It...*www.superquicklessons.com/cheese

International Bestsellers by John C. Maxwell

Be A People Person
*Buy It...*www.superquicklessons.com/peopleperson

25 Ways To Win With People
How To Make Others Feel Like A Million Bucks
*Buy It...*www.superquicklessons.com/winpeople

Developing The Leader Within You
*Buy It...*www.superquicklessons.com/leaderyou

Developing The Leaders Around You
*Buy It...*www.superquicklessons.com/aroundyou

21 Irrefutable Laws Of Leadership
Follow Them and People Will Follow You
*Buy It...*www.superquicklessons.com/21laws

Becoming A Person Of Influence
*Buy It...*www.superquicklessons.com/influence

Be All You Can Be
*Buy It...*www.superquicklessons.com/beall

Randy's SuperQuickRecommendations™

International Bestsellers by Napoleon Hill

Think and Grow Rich
*Buy It...*www.superquicklessons.com/thinkrich

The Law of Success 21st Century Edition
*Buy It...*www.superquicklessons.com/successlaw

The Science of Personal Achievement
(audio series)
*Buy It...*www.superquicklessons.com/science

International Bestsellers by Al Ries

The 22 Immutable Laws of Marketing
*Buy It...*www.superquicklessons.com/immutable

The Fall of Advertising and the Rise of PR.
*Buy It...*www.superquicklessons.com/thefall

Personal Favorites

Getting, Keeping, and Deserving Your Customers
Audio program by Patricia Fripp, CSP, CPAE
Buy It... www.superquicklessons.com/fripp

The Ultimate Guide to Electronic Marketing for Small Business
Best Selling book by Tom Antion
Buy It... www.superquicklessons.com/ultimate

Butt Camp
Elelctronic Marketing for Small Business
Audio Program by Tom Antion
Buy It... www.superquicklessons.com/buttcamp

The Great Internet Marketing Mentor Program
12 month Mentoring Program with Tom Antion
Buy It... www.superquicklessons.com/mentor

Boost Business with Your Own E-zine Study Course
by the "E-zine Queen" Alexandria K. Brown
Buy it... www.superquicklessons.com/ezinequeen

Personal Favorites

The Power of Outrageous Marketing!

Using the 10 Time-Tested Secrets of Titans, Tycoons, And Billionaires to get Rich in your Own Business.

Audio Program by Joe "Mr. Fire" Vitale

Buy it...www.superquicklessons.com/mrfire

Beyond WOW!

*book by Myra Golden
& Dr. Jeffrey Magee*

Buy It...www.superquicklessons.com/wow

**The Ultimate Customer Recovery Guidebook:
How to Keep Customers Coming Back
After a Service Mishap**
E-book by Myra Golden

Buy It...www.superquicklessons.com/comeback

Masters of Networking

book by Ivan R. Misner, Ph.D.& Don Morgan M.A.

Buy It...www.superquicklessons.com/mastersnet

Zapp!

*The Lightning Of Empowerment
Bestselling book by William C. Byham*

Buy It...www.superquicklessons.com/zapp

Carpe Aqualis!

"Seize the Wave"

Bestselling book by Frank F. Lunn

Buy It...www.superquicklessons.com/carpe

About the Author

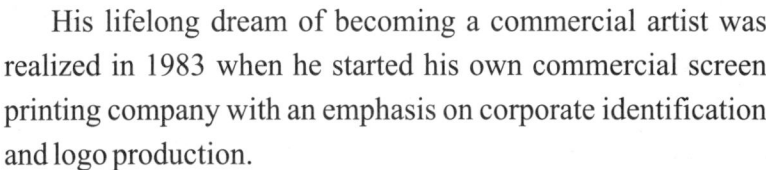

Randy Clay was born and raised in Tulsa, Oklahoma.

His lifelong dream of becoming a commercial artist was realized in 1983 when he started his own commercial screen printing company with an emphasis on corporate identification and logo production.

U.S. SafetySign & Decal is now a leading manufacturer of all types of OSHA compliant signs for the oil and gas industries.

His writing and public speaking include various subjects that communicate positive attitude and reaching your personal potential.

His desire, wherever he goes, is to help people realize they are born with a mission to accomplish something great.

Randy and his wife Melanie are raising two future business investors, Joshua and Caleb, and live in Sand Springs, Oklahoma, a suburb of Tulsa.

Randy can be easily reached through his website and now has a free e-zine to anyone wanting to continue their business education.

The website address is *www.superquicklessons.com.*

Website

SuperQuickLessons.com ™

Randy's Bio

Products

Public Speaker

Randy's Personal Blog

Entrepreneur, Author, and Public Speaker Randy Clay recognized the reality of the following statistic 90% of all new businesses either drown in their ignorance or business finance or are eaten alive for lack of business skills within the first five years.

Whether you have a product or service business, *SuperQuickLessons* E-zine will give you the information to beat the odds. Every issue will have a featured article from either Randy and his over 20 years of business experience or the insight of one of his Information Masters.

SuperQuickLessons
E-Zine *Randy Clay*

Name

E-mail

FREE

Subscribe

Speaking Topics

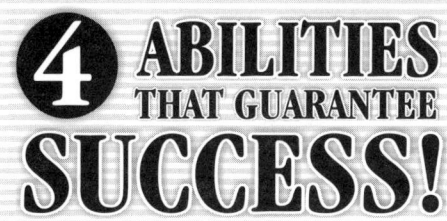 

NOW
AVAILABLE ON
DVD VIDEO
www.superquicklessons.com

There Are 4 Simple Abilities that most corporations are looking for in addition to your professional skills.

Chances are, your college or university forgot to remind you of them!

Other Great Topics

Is Your Networking, NOT-working?

SAFETY
SIGN LANGUAGE

For information about booking Randy for your next event call 800-750-2529

Randy's

SuperQuickOrderInfo

To order more copies of this book call

1-800-750-2529

Have your credit card ready.
Remember to ask for quantity discounts.

To order any of the books or products
mentioned in this book go to our website.
You'll find the accurate address to enter, under
each product Randy recommended.

To book Randy for your next organizational
event call 1-800-750-2529
or email *amy@superquicklessons.com*

To subscribe to

SuperQuickLessons
E-Zine *Randy Clay*

go to www.superquicklessons.com
It's FREE!